THE HEROES

See page 11

'PERSEUS, DARE YUO FACE SUCH A MONSTER AS THIS
AND SLAY IT?'

THE HEROES

by

CHARLES KINGSLEY

*Illustrated with four colour plates
and line drawings in the text by*
JOAN KIDDELL-MONROE

LONDON: J. M. DENT & SONS LTD
NEW YORK: E. P. DUTTON & CO. INC.

CHARLES KINGSLEY, *novelist and historian, was born on 12th June 1819 at Holne, on the edge of Dartmoor. His childhood was divided between Barnack in the Fen country (the scene of 'Hereward the Wake') and Clovelly near Bideford in Devon (the setting for 'Westward Ho!'). He was educated at King's College, London, and Magdalene College, Cambridge, entered the Church, and became rector of Eversley in Hampshire. He was Professor of Modern History at Cambridge, 1860–9, and was made a canon of Chester in 1869 and of Westminster in 1873. He died on 23rd January 1875.*

Kingsley was a minor poet of distinction : his best known poem, 'The Sands of Dee', commemorates the Cheshire home of his medieval ancestors, who were hereditary Foresters of Delamere. As a novelist he missed greatness only by the instability of his temperament, which caused him to sacrifice his literary skill to his crusade of the moment. 'Yeast' (1848) begins as a great novel and ends as an anti-Catholic tract. He was more successful in his historical romances, of which 'Westward Ho!' (1855), still the most popular, was freest from his besetting fault. His most famous book, a fantasy for children called 'The Water Babies' (1863), though by no means free from arbitrary didacticism and avuncularism, is a work of genius which has captivated children and repelled adults for a hundred years. His most completely successful work is 'The Heroes' (1856), a retelling for his own children of three of the greatest of the ancient Greek legends: it is undoubtedly the finest book of its kind published in the nineteenth century, and it is still unsurpassed.

ISBN: 0 460 05058 3

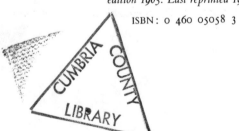

AUTHOR'S PREFACE

To

My children, Rose, Maurice and Mary
a little present of old Greek Fairy Tales

MY DEAR CHILDREN,—Some of you have heard already of the old Greeks; and all of you, as you grow up, will hear more and more of them. Those of you who are boys will, perhaps, spend a great deal of time in reading Greek books; and the girls, though they may not learn Greek, will be sure to come across a great many stories taken from Greek history, and to see, I may say every day, things which we should not have had it if had not been for these old Greeks. You can hardly find a well-written book which has not in it Greek names, and words, and proverbs; you cannot walk through a great town without passing Greek buildings; you cannot go into a well-furnished room without seeing Greek statues and ornaments, even Greek patterns of furniture and paper; so strangely have these old Greeks left their mark behind them upon this modern world in which we now live. And as you grow up, and read more and more, you will find that we owe to these old Greeks the beginnings of all our mathematics and geometry—that is, the science and knowledge of numbers, and of the shapes of things, and of the forces which make things move and stand at rest; and the beginnings of our geography and astronomy; and of our laws, and freedom, and politics—that is, the science of how to rule a country, and make it peaceful and strong. And we owe to them, too, the beginning of our logic—that is, the study of words and of reasoning; and of our metaphysics—that is, the study of our own thoughts and souls. And last of all, they made their language so beautiful that foreigners used to take to it instead of their own; and at last Greek became the common language of educated people all over the old world, from Persia and Egypt even to Spain and Britain. And therefore it was that the New Testament was written in Greek, that it might be read and understood by all the nations of the Roman Empire; so that, next to the Jews, and the Bible which the Jews handed down to us, we owe more to these old Greeks than to any people upon earth.

Now you must remember one thing—that 'Greeks' was not their real name. They called themselves always 'Hellenes', but the Romans miscalled them Greeks; and we have taken that wrong name from the Romans—it would take a long time to tell you why. They were made up of many tribes and many small separate states; and when you hear in this book of Minyai, and Athenians, and other such names, you must remember that they were all different tribes and peoples of the one great Hellene race, who lived in what we now call Greece, in the islands of the Archipelago, and along the coast of Asia Minor (Ionia, as they call it), from the Hellespont to Rhodes, and had afterwards colonies and cities in Sicily, and South Italy (which was called Great Greece), and along the shores of the Black Sea, at Sinope, and Kertch, and at Sevastopol. And after that, again, they spread under Alexander the Great, and conquered Egypt, and Syria, and Persia, and the whole East. But that was many hundred years after my stories; for then there were no Greeks on the Black Sea shores, nor in Sicily, or Italy, or anywhere but in Greece and in Ionia. And if you are puzzled by the names of places in this book, you must take the maps and find them out. It will be a pleasanter way of learning geography than out of a dull lesson-book.

Now, I love these old Hellenes heartily; and I should be very ungrateful to them if I did not, considering all that they have taught me; and they seem to me like brothers, though they have all been dead and gone many hundred years ago. So as you must learn about them, whether you choose or not, I wish to be the first to introduce you to them, and to say: 'Come hither, children, at this blessed Christmas time, when all God's creatures should rejoice together, and bless Him who redeemed them all. Come and see old friends of mine, whom I knew long ere you were born. They are come to visit us at Christmas, out of the world where all live to God; and to tell you some of their old fairy-tales, which they loved when they were young like you.'

For nations begin at first by being children like you, though they are made up of grown men. They are children at first like you— men and women with children's hearts; frank, and affectionate, and full of trust, and teachable, and loving to see and learn all the wonders round them; and greedy also, too often, and passionate and silly, as children are.

Thus these old Greeks were teachable, and learnt from all the nations round. From the Phoenicians they learnt shipbuilding, and some say letters beside; and from the Assyrians they learnt painting, and carving, and building in wood and stone; and from the Egyptians they learnt astronomy, and many things which you would not understand. In this they were like our own forefathers the Northmen, of whom you love to hear, who, though they were wild and rough themselves, were humble, and glad to learn from everyone. Therefore God rewarded these Greeks, as He rewarded our forefathers, and made them wiser than the people who taught them in everything they learnt; for He loves to see men and children openhearted, and willing to be taught; and to him who uses what he has got, He gives more and more day by day. So these Greeks grew wise and powerful, and wrote poems which will live till the world's end, which you must read for yourselves some day, in English at least, if not in Greek. And they learnt to carve statues, and build temples, which are still among the wonders of the world; and many another wondrous thing God taught them, for which we are the wiser this day.

Now, you must not think of them in this book as learned men, living in great cities, such as they were afterwards, when they wrought all their beautiful works, but as country people, living in farms and walled villages, in a simple, hardworking way, so that the greatest kings and heroes cooked their own meals, and thought it no shame, and made their own ships and weapons, and fed and harnessed their own horses; and the queens worked with their maidservants, and did all the business of the house, and spun, and wove, and embroidered, and made their husbands' clothes and their own. So that a man was honoured among them, not because he happened to be rich, but according to his skill, and his strength and courage, and the number of things which he could do. For they were but grown-up children, though they were right noble children too; and it was with them as it is now at school—the strongest and cleverest boy, though he be poor, leads all the rest.

Now, while they were young and simple they loved fairy-tales, as you do now. All nations do so when they are young: our old forefathers did, and called their stories 'Sagas'. I will read you some of them some day—some of the Eddas, and the Voluspà, and Beowulf, and the noble old Romances. The old Arabs, again, had their tales, which we now call the 'Arabian Nights'. The old Romans had theirs, and they called them 'Fabulae', from which our word 'fable' comes; but the old Hellenes called theirs 'Muthoi', from which our new word 'myth' is taken. But next to those old Romances, which were written in the Christian middle age, there are no fairy-tales like these old Greek ones, for beauty, and wisdom, and truth, and for making children love noble deeds, and trust in God to help them through.

Now, why have I called this book *The Heroes*? Because that was the name which the Hellenes gave to men who were brave and skilful, and dare do more than other men. At first, I think, that was all it meant; but after a time it came to mean something more: it came to mean men who helped their country; men in those old times, when the country was half wild, who killed fierce beasts and evil men, and drained swamps, and founded towns, and therefore after they were dead, were honoured, because they had left their country better than they found it. And we call such a man a hero in English to this day, and call it a 'heroic' thing to suffer pain and grief, that we may do good to our fellow men. We may all do that, my children, boys and girls alike; and we ought to do it, for it is easier now than ever, and safer, and the path more clear. But you shall hear how the Hellenes said their heroes worked, three thousand years ago. The stories are not all true, of course, nor half of them; you are not simple enough to fancy that; but the meaning of them is true, and true for ever, and that is—'Do right, and God will help you.'

FARLEY COURT,
    Advent, 1855

CONTENTS

ILLUSTRATIONS

IN COLOUR

Perseus

PART I

How Perseus and his Mother Came to Seriphos

ONCE UPON a time there were two princes who were twins. Their names were Acrisius and Proetus, and they lived in the pleasant vale of Argos, far away in Hellas. They had fruitful meadows and vineyards, sheep and oxen, great herds of horses feeding down in Lerna Fen, and all that men could need to make them blest: and yet they were wretched, because they were jealous of each other. From the moment they were born they began to quarrel; and when they grew up each tried to take away the other's share of the kingdom, and keep all for himself. So first Acrisius drove out Proetus, and he went across the seas and brought home a foreign princess for his wife and foreign warriors to help him, who were called Cyclopes; and drove out Acrisius in his turn; and then they fought a long while up and down the land, till the quarrel was settled, and Acrisius took Argos and one half the land, and Proetus took Tiryns and the other half. And

Proetus and his Cyclopes built around Tiryns great walls of unhewn stone, which are standing to this day.

But there came a prophet to that hard-hearted Acrisius and prophesied against him, and said: 'Because you have risen up against your own blood, your own blood shall rise up against you; because you have sinned against your kindred, by your kindred you shall be punished. Your daughter Danaë shall bear a son, and by that son's hands you shall die. So the gods have ordained, and it will surely come to pass.'

And at that Acrisius was very much afraid; but he did not mend his ways. He had been cruel to his own family, and instead of repenting and being kind to them, he went on to be more cruel than ever: for he shut up his fair daughter Danaë in a cavern underground, lined with brass, that no one might come near her. So he fancied himself more cunning than the gods: but you will see presently whether he was able to escape them.

Now it came to pass that in time Danaë bore a son—so beautiful a babe that any but King Acrisius would have had pity on it. But he had no pity; for he took Danaë and her babe down to the seashore, and put them into a great chest and thrust them out to sea, for the winds and the waves to carry them whithersoever they would.

The north-west wind blew freshly out of the blue mountains and down the pleasant vale of Argos, and away and out to sea. And away and out to sea before it floated the mother and her babe, while all who watched them wept, save that cruel father, King Acrisius.

So they floated on and on, and the chest danced up and down upon the billows, and the baby slept upon its mother's breast:

but the poor mother could not sleep, but watched and wept, and she sang to her baby as they floated; and the song which she sang you shall learn yourselves some day.

And now they are past the last blue headland and in the open sea; and there is nothing round them but the waves and the sky and the wind. But the waves are gentle and the sky is clear and the breeze is tender and low; for these are the days when Halcyone and Ceyx build their nests, and no storms ever ruffle the pleasant summer sea.

And who were Halcyone and Ceyx? You shall hear while the chest floats on. Halcyone was a fairy maiden, the daughter of the beach and of the wind. And she loved a sailor boy and married him; and none on earth were so happy as they. But at last Ceyx was wrecked; and before he could swim to the shore the billows swallowed him up. And Halcyone saw him drowning, and leapt into the sea to him; but in vain. Then the Immortals took pity on them both, and changed them into two fair sea-birds; and now they build a floating nest every year and sail up and down happily for ever upon the pleasant seas of Greece.

So a night passed, and a day—and a long day it was for Danaë; and another night and day beside, till Danaë was faint with hunger and weeping, and yet no land appeared. And all the while the babe slept quietly; and at last poor Danaë drooped her head and fell asleep likewise with her cheek against the babe's.

After a while she was awakened suddenly; for the chest was jarring and grinding, and the air was full of sound. She looked up, and over her head were mighty cliffs, all red in the setting sun, and around her rocks and breakers and flying flakes of foam. She clasped her hands together and shrieked aloud for help. And when she cried, help met her: for now there came over the rocks a tall and stately man, and he looked down wondering upon poor Danaë tossing about in the chest among the waves.

He wore a rough cloak of frieze and on his head a broad hat to shade his face; in his hand he carried a trident for spearing fish, and over his shoulder was a casting-net. But Danaë could see that he was no common man by his stature and his walk and his flowing golden hair and beard, and by the two servants who came behind him, carrying baskets for his fish. But she had hardly time to look at him before he had laid aside his trident and leapt down the rocks and thrown his casting-net so surely over Danaë and the chest, that he drew it and her and the baby, safe upon a ledge of rock.

Then the fisherman took Danaë by the hand, and lifted her out of the chest, and said:

'O beautiful damsel, what strange chance has brought you to this island in so frail a ship? Who are you, and whence? Surely you are some king's daughter; and this boy has some-what more than mortal.'

And as he spoke he pointed to the babe; for its face shone like the morning star.

But Danaë only held down her head, and sobbed out:

'Tell me to what land I have come, unhappy that I am; and among what men I have fallen!'

And he said: 'This isle is called Seriphos, and I am a Hellene, and dwell in it. I am the brother of Polydectes the king; and men call me Dictys the netter, because I catch the fish of the shore.'

Then Danaë fell down at his feet, and embraced his knees and cried:

'Oh, sir, have pity upon a stranger, whom a cruel doom has driven to your land, and let me live in your house as a servant; but treat me honourably, for I was once a king's daughter, and this my boy (as you have truly said) is of no common race. I will not be a charge to you, or eat the bread of idleness; for I am more skilful in weaving and embroidery than all the maidens of my land.'

And she was going on; but Dictys stopped her and raised her up, and said:

'My daughter, I am old, and my hairs are growing grey, while I have no children to make my home cheerful. Come with me then and you shall be a daughter to me and to my wife, and this babe shall be our grandchild. For I fear the gods and show hospitality to all strangers, knowing that good deeds, like evil ones, always return to those who do them.'

So Danaë was comforted and went home with Dictys the good fisherman and was a daughter to him and to his wife till fifteen years were past.

PART II

How Perseus Vowed a Rash Vow

FIFTEEN years were past and gone, and the babe was now grown to be a tall lad and a sailor, and went many voyages after merchandise to the islands round. His mother called him Perseus; but all the people in Seriphos said that he was not the son of mortal man, and called him the son of Zeus, the king of the Immortals. For though he was but fifteen, he was taller by a head than any man in the island; and he was the most skilful of all in running and wrestling and boxing, and in throwing the quoit and the javelin, and in rowing with the oar, and in playing on the harp, and in all which befits a man. And he was brave and truthful, gentle and courteous; for good old Dictys had trained him well—and

well it was for Perseus that he had done so. For now Danaë
and her son fell into great danger, and Perseus had need of all
his wit to defend his mother and himself.

I said that Dictys' brother was Polydectes, king of the
island. He was not a righteous man, like Dictys, but greedy
and cunning and cruel. And when he saw fair Danaë, he
wanted to marry her. But she would not; for she did not love
him, and cared for no one but her boy and her boy's father,
whom she never hoped to see again. At last Polydectes became
furious, and while Perseus was away at sea he took poor Danaë
away from Dictys, saying: 'If you will not be my wife, you
shall be my slave.' So Danaë was made a slave, and had to fetch
water from the well, and grind in the mill, and perhaps was
beaten, and made to wear a heavy chain, because she would not
marry that cruel king. But Perseus was far away over the seas
in the isle of Samos, little thinking how his mother was lan-
guishing in grief.

Now one day at Samos while the ship was lading, Perseus
wandered into a pleasant wood to get out of the sun, and sat
down on the turf and fell asleep. And as he slept a strange
dream came to him—the strangest dream which he had ever
had in his life.

There came a lady to him through the wood, taller than he
or any mortal man, but beautiful exceedingly, with great grey
eyes, clear and piercing, but strangely soft and mild. On her
head was a helmet and in her hand a spear. And over her
shoulder above her long blue robes hung a goatskin, which
bore up a mighty shield of brass, polished like a mirror. She
stood and looked at him with her clear grey eyes; and Perseus
saw that her eyelids never moved, nor her eyeballs, but looked

straight through and through him, and into his very heart, as
if she could see all the secrets of his soul, and knew all that he
had ever thought or longed for since the day that he was born.
And Perseus dropped his eyes, trembling and blushing, as the
wonderful lady spoke.

'Perseus, you must do an errand for me.'

'Who are you, lady? And how do you know my
name?'

'I am Pallas Athené; and I know the thoughts of all men's
hearts, and discern their manhood or their baseness. And from
the souls of clay I turn away, and they are blest, but not by me.
They fatten at ease, like sheep in the pasture, and eat what they
did not sow, like oxen in the stall. They grow and spread, like
the gourd along the ground; but like the gourd they give no
shade to the traveller, and when they are ripe, death gathers
them, and they go down unloved into hell, and their name
vanishes out of the land.

'But to the souls of fire I give more fire, and to those who are
manly I give a might more than man's. These are the heroes,
the sons of the Immortals, who are blest, but not like the souls
of clay. For I drive them forth by strange paths, Perseus, that
they may fight the Titans and the monsters, the enemies of gods
and men. Through doubt and need, danger and battle, I drive
them; and some of them are slain in the flower of youth, no
man knows when or where; and some of them win noble
names, and a fair and green old age. But what will be their
latter end I know not, and none, save Zeus, the father of gods
and men. Tell me now, Perseus, which of these two sorts of
men seem to you more blest?'

Then Perseus answered boldly: 'Better to die in the flower

of youth on the chance of winning a noble name, than to live at ease like the sheep, and die unloved and unrenowned.'

Then that strange lady laughed, and held up her brazen shield, and cried: 'See here, Perseus; dare you face such a monster as this and slay it, that I may place its head upon this shield?'

And in the mirror of the shield there appeared a face, and as Perseus looked on it his blood ran cold. It was the face of a beautiful woman, but her cheeks were pale as death and her brows were knit with everlasting pain and her lips were thin and bitter like a snake's; and instead of hair, vipers wreathed about her temples and shot out their forked tongues, while round her head were folded wings like an eagle's, and upon her bosom claws of brass.

And Perseus looked awhile, and then said: 'If there is anything so fierce and foul on earth, it were a noble deed to kill it. Where can I find the monster?'

Then the strange lady smiled again, and said: 'Not yet; you are too young and too unskilled; for this is Medusa the Gorgon, the mother of a monstrous brood. Return to your home and do the work which waits there for you. You must play the man in that before I can think you worthy to go in search of the Gorgon.'

Then Perseus would have spoken, but the strange lady vanished and he awoke; and behold, it was a dream. But day and night Perseus saw before him the face of that dreadful woman, with the vipers writhing round her head.

So he returned home; and when he came to Seriphos, the first thing which he heard was that his mother was a slave in the house of Polydectes.

Grinding his teeth with rage, he went out and away to the king's palace and through the men's rooms and the women's rooms, and so through all the house (for no one dared stop him, so terrible and fair was he) till he found his mother sitting on the floor, turning the stone hand-mill, and weeping as she turned it. And he lifted her up and kissed her and bade her follow him forth. But before they could pass out of the room Polydectes came in, raging. And when Perseus saw him, he flew upon him as the mastiff flies on the boar. 'Villain and tyrant!' he cried. 'Is this your respect for the gods, and your mercy to strangers and widows? You shall die!' And because he had no sword he caught up the stone hand-mill and lifted it to dash out Polydectes' brains.

But his mother clung to him, shrieking: 'Oh, my son, we are strangers and helpless in the land; and if you kill the king, all the people will fall on us, and we shall both die.'

Good Dictys too who had come in, entreated him: 'Remember that he is my brother. Remember how I have brought you up and trained you as my own son, and spare him for my sake.'

Then Perseus lowered his hand; and Polydectes, who had been trembling all this while like a coward because he knew that he was in the wrong, let Perseus and his mother pass.

Perseus took his mother to the temple of Athené, and there the priestess made her one of the temple-sweepers; for there they knew she would be safe, and not even Polydectes would dare to drag her away from the altar. And there Perseus and the good Dictys and his wife came to visit her every day, while Polydectes, not being able to get what he wanted by force, cast about in his wicked heart how he might get it by cunning.

Now he was sure that he could never get back Danaë as long as Perseus was in the island; so he made a plot to rid himself of him. And first he pretended to have forgiven Perseus and to have forgotten Danaë, so that for a while all went as smoothly as ever.

Next he proclaimed a great feast, and invited to it all the chiefs and landowners and the young men of the island, and

among them Perseus, that they might all do him homage as their king and eat of his banquet in his hall.

On the appointed day they all came; and as the custom was then, each guest brought his present with him to the king: one a horse, another a shawl or a ring or a sword; and those who had nothing better brought a basket of grapes or of game. But Perseus brought nothing, for he had nothing to bring, being but a poor sailor-lad.

He was ashamed, however, to go into the king's presence without his gift, and he was too proud to ask Dictys to lend him one. So he stood at the door sorrowfully, watching the rich men go in; and his face grew very red as they pointed at him and smiled and whispered: 'What has that foundling to give?'

Now this was what Polydectes wanted; and as soon as he heard that Perseus stood without, he bade them bring him in, and asked him scornfully before them all: 'Am I not your king, Perseus, and have I not invited you to my feast? Where is your present then?'

Perseus blushed and stammered, while all the proud men round laughed, and some of them began jeering him openly. 'This fellow was thrown ashore here like a piece of weed or driftwood, and yet he is too proud to bring a gift to the king.'

'And though he does not know who his father is, he is vain enough to let the old women call him the son of Zeus.'

And so forth, till poor Perseus grew mad with shame, and hardly knowing what he said, cried out: 'A present! Who are you who talk of presents? See if I do not bring a nobler one than all of yours together!'

So he said boasting; and yet he felt in his heart that he was braver than all those scoffers, and more able to do some glorious deed.

'Hear him! Hear the boaster! What is it to be?' cried they all, laughing louder than ever.

Then his dream at Samos came into his mind, and he cried aloud: 'The head of the Gorgon.'

He was half afraid after he had said the words; for all laughed louder than ever, and Polydectes loudest of all.

'You have promised to bring me the Gorgon's head? Then never appear again in this island without it. Go!'

Perseus ground his teeth with rage, for he saw that he had fallen into a trap; but his promise lay upon him, and he went out without a word.

Down to the cliffs he went, and looked across the broad

blue sea; and he wondered if his dream were true, and prayed in the bitterness of his soul:

'Pallas Athené, was my dream true? And shall I slay the Gorgon? If thou didst really show me her face, let me not come to shame as a liar and boastful. Rashly and angrily I promised; but cunningly and patiently will I perform.'

But there was no answer, nor sign; neither thunder nor any appearance; not even a cloud in the sky.

And three times Perseus called weeping, 'Rashly and angrily I promised; but cunningly and patiently will I perform.'

Then he saw afar off above the sea a small white cloud, as bright as silver. And it came on, nearer and nearer, till its brightness dazzled his eyes.

Perseus wondered at that strange cloud, for there was no other cloud all round the sky; and he trembled as it touched the cliff below. And as it touched it broke and parted, and within it appeared Pallas Athené, as he had seen her at Samos in his dream, and beside her a young man more light-limbed than the stag, whose eyes were like sparks of fire. By his side was a sword of diamond, all of one clear precious stone, and on his feet were golden sandals, from the heels of which grew living wings.

They looked upon Perseus keenly, and yet they never moved their eyes; and they came up the cliffs towards him more swiftly than the seagull, and yet they never moved their feet, nor did the breeze stir the robes about their limbs; only the wings of the youth's sandals quivered, like a hawk's when he hangs above the cliff. And Perseus fell down and worshipped, for he knew that they were more than man.

But Athené stood before him and spoke gently, and bid him have no fear. Then:

'Perseus,' she said, 'he who overcomes in one trial merits thereby a sharper trial still. You have braved Polydectes, and done manfully. Dare you brave Medusa the Gorgon?'

And Perseus said: 'Try me; for since you spoke to me in Samos a new soul has come into my breast, and I should be ashamed not to dare anything which I can do. Show me then how I can do this!'

'Perseus,' said Athené, 'think well before you attempt; for this deed requires a seven years' journey in which you cannot repent or turn back nor escape; but if your heart fails you, you must die in the Unshapen Land, where no man will ever find your bones.'

'Better so than live here useless and despised,' said Perseus. 'Tell me then, oh tell me, fair and wise goddess, of your great kindness and condescension, how I can do but this one thing, and then, if need be, die!'

Then Athené smiled and said:

'Be patient and listen; for if you forget my words, you will indeed die. You must go northward to the country of the Hyperboreans, who live beyond the pole, at the sources of the cold north wind, till you find the three Grey Sisters, who have but one eye and one tooth between them. You must ask them the way to the nymphs, the daughters of the Evening Star, who dance about the golden tree in the Atlantic island of the west. They will tell you the way to the Gorgon, that you may slay her, my enemy, the mother of monstrous beasts. Once she was a maiden as beautiful as morn, till in her pride she sinned a sin at which the sun hid his face. And from that day her hair was turned to vipers, and her hands to eagle's claws, and her heart was filled with shame and rage, and her lips with bitter venom; and her eyes became so terrible that whosoever looks on them is turned to stone; and her children are the winged horse and the giant of the golden sword; and her grandchildren are Echidna the witch-adder and Geryon the three-headed tyrant, who feeds his herds beside the herds of hell. So she became the sister of the Gorgons, Stheino and Euryte the abhorred, the daughters of the Queen of the Sea. Touch them not, for they are immortal; but bring me only Medusa's head.'

'And I will bring it!' said Perseus. 'But how am I to escape her eyes? Will she not freeze me too into stone?'

'You shall take this polished shield,' said Athené, 'and when you come near her look not at her herself, but at her image in the brass; so you may strike her safely. And when you have struck off her head, wrap it, with your face turned away, in the folds of the goatskin on which the shield hangs, the hide of Amaltheié, the nurse of the Aegisholder. So you will bring it safely back to me and win to yourself renown and a place among the heroes who feast with the Immortals upon the peak where no winds blow.'

Then Perseus said: 'I will go, though I die in going. But how shall I cross the seas without a ship? And who will show me my way? And when I find her, how shall I slay her, if her scales be iron and brass?'

Then the young man spoke: 'These sandals of mine will bear you across the seas, and over hill and dale like a bird, as they bear me all day long; for I am Hermes, the far-famed Argus-slayer, the messenger of the Immortals who dwell on Olympus.'

Then Perseus fell down and worshipped, while the young man spoke again:

'The sandals themselves will guide you on the road, for they are divine and cannot stray; and this sword itself, the Argus-slayer, will kill her, for it is divine and needs no second stroke. Arise and gird them on and go forth.'

So Perseus arose, and girded on the sandals and the sword.

And Athené cried: 'Now leap from the cliff and be gone.'

But Perseus lingered.

'May I not bid farewell to my mother and to Dictys? And may I not offer burnt-offerings to you, and to Hermes the far-famed Argus-slayer, and to Father Zeus above?'

'You shall not bid farewell to your mother, lest your heart relent at her weeping. I will comfort her and Dictys until you return in peace. Nor shall you offer burnt-offerings to the Olympians; for your offering shall be Medusa's head. Leap, and trust in the armour of the Immortals.'

Then Perseus looked down the cliff and shuddered; but he was ashamed to show his dread. Then he thought of Medusa and the renown before him, and he leapt into the empty air.

And behold, instead of falling he floated and stood and ran along the sky. He looked back, but Athené had vanished, and Hermes; and the sandals led him on northward ever, like a crane who follows the spring toward the Ister [1] fens.

---

[1] The Danube.

PART III

How Perseus Slew the Gorgon

So Perseus started on his journey, going dry-shod over land and sea; and his heart was high and joyful, for the winged sandals bore him each day a seven days' journey. And he went by Cythnus and by Ceos and the pleasant Cyclades to Attica, and past Athens and Thebes and the Copaic lake and up the vale of Cephissus and past the peaks of Oeta and Pindus and over the rich Thessalian plains, till the sunny hills of Greece were behind him and before him were the wilds of the north. Then he passed the Thracian mountains and many a barbarous tribe, Paeons and Dardans and Triballi, till he came to the Ister stream, and the dreary Scythian plains. And he walked across the Ister dry-shod, and away through the moors and fens day and night, toward the bleak north-west, turning neither to the right hand nor the left, till he came to the Unshapen Land, and the place which has no name.

And seven days he walked through it, on a path which few can tell; for those who have trodden it like least to speak of it, and those who go there again in dreams are glad enough when they awake; till he came to the edge of the everlasting night, where the air was full of feathers and the soil was hard with ice, and there at last he found the three Grey Sisters, by the shore of the freezing sea, nodding upon a white log of driftwood, beneath the cold white winter moon; and they chaunted a low song together: 'Why the old times were better than the new.'

There was no living thing around them, not a fly, not a moss upon the rocks. Neither seal nor seagull dare come near, lest the ice should clutch them in its claws. The surge broke up in foam, but it fell again in flakes of snow, and it frosted the hair of the three Grey Sisters and the bones in the ice-cliff above their heads. They passed the eye from one to the other, but for all that they could not see; and they passed the tooth from one to the other, but for all that they could not eat; and they sat in the full glare of the moon, but they were none the warmer for her beams. And Perseus pitied the three Grey Sisters, but they did not pity themselves.

So he said: 'Oh, venerable mothers, wisdom is the daughter of old age. You therefore should know many things. Tell me, if you can, the path to the Gorgon.'

Then one cried: 'Who is this who reproaches us with old age?' And another: 'This is the voice of one of the children of men.'

And he: 'I do not reproach, but honour your old age, and I am one of the sons of men and of the heroes. The rulers of Olympus have sent me to you to ask the way to the Gorgon.'

Then one: 'There are new rulers in Olympus, and all new

things are bad.' And another: 'We hate your rulers and the heroes and all the children of men. We are the kindred of the Titans and the Giants and the Gorgons and the ancient monsters of the deep.' And another: 'Who is this rash and insolent man who pushes unbidden into our world?' And the first: 'There never was such a word as ours, nor will be: if we let him see it, he will spoil it all.'

Then one cried: 'Give me the eye, that I may see him'; and another: 'Give me the tooth, that I may bite him.' But Perseus, when he saw that they were foolish and proud, and did not love the children of men, left off pitying them and said to himself: 'Hungry men must needs be hasty; if I stay making many words here, I shall be starved.' Then he stepped close to them and watched till they passed the eye from hand to hand. And as they groped about between themselves, he held out his own hand gently, till one of them put the eye into it, fancying that it was the hand of her sister. Then he sprang back, and laughed, and cried:

'Cruel and proud old women, I have your eye; and I will throw it into the sea, unless you tell me the path to the Gorgon, and swear to me that you tell me right.'

They they wept and chattered and scolded; but in vain. They were forced to tell the truth, though when they told it Perseus could hardly make out the road.

'You must go,' they said, 'foolish boy, to the southward into the ugly glare of the sun, till you come to Atlas the giant who holds the heavens and the earth apart. And you must ask his daughters, the Hesperides, who are young and foolish like yourself. And now give us back our eye, for we have forgotten all the rest.'

So Perseus gave them back their eye; but instead of using it, they nodded and fell fast asleep and were turned into blocks of ice, till the tide came up and washed them all away. And now they float up and down like icebergs for ever, weeping whenever they meet the sunshine and the fruitful summer and the warm south wind which fill young hearts with joy.

But Perseus leapt away to the southward, leaving the snow and ice behind, past the isle of the Hyperboreans and the tin isles and the long Iberian shore, while the sun rose higher day by day upon a bright blue summer sea. And the terns and the seagulls swept laughing round his head and called to him to stop and play, and the dolphins gambolled up as he passed and offered to carry him on their backs. And all night long the sea-nymphs sang sweetly, and the Tritons blew upon their conchs as they played round Galataea their queen in her car of pearled shells. Day by day the sun rose higher and leapt more swiftly into the sea at night and more swiftly out of the sea at dawn, while Perseus skimmed over the billows like a seagull, and his feet were never wetted; and leapt on from wave to wave, and his limbs were never weary, till he saw far away a mighty mountain, all rose-red in the setting sun. Its feet were wrapped in forests, and its head in wreaths of cloud; and Perseus knew that it was Atlas, who holds the heavens and the earth apart.

He came to the mountain and leapt on shore and wandered upward among pleasant valleys and waterfalls and tall trees and strange ferns and flowers; but there was no smoke rising from any glen, nor house, nor sign of man.

At last he heard sweet voices singing; and he guessed that he was come to the garden of the nymphs, the daughters of the Evening Star.

They sang like nightingales among the thickets, and Perseus
stopped to hear their song; but the words which they spoke he
could not understand—no, nor no man after him for many a hundred years. So he stepped forward and saw them dancing, hand
in hand, around the charmed tree which bent under its golden
fruit; and round the tree-foot was coiled the dragon, old Ladon
the sleepless snake, who lies there for ever, listening to the song
of the maidens, blinking and watching with dry bright eyes.

Then Perseus stopped, not because he feared the dragon, but
because he was bashful before those fair maids; but when they
saw him, they too stopped, and called to him with trembling
voices:

'Who are you? Are you Heracles the mighty, who will come
to rob our garden, and carry off our golden fruit?' And he
answered:

'I am not Heracles the mighty, and I want none of your golden fruit. Tell me, fair nymphs, the way which leads to the Gorgon, that I may go on my way and slay her.'

'Not yet, not yet, fair boy; come dance with us around the tree in the garden which knows no winter, the home of the south wind and the sun. Come hither and play with us awhile; we have danced alone here for a thousand years, and our hearts are weary with longing for a playfellow. So come, come, come!'

'I cannot dance with you, fair maidens; for I must do the errand of the Immortals. So tell me the way to the Gorgon lest I wander and perish in the waves.'

Then they sighed and wept, and answered:

'The Gorgon! She will freeze you into stone.'

'It is better to die like a hero than to live like an ox in a stall. The Immortals have lent me weapons, and they will give me wit to use them.'

Then they sighed again and answered: 'Fair boy, if you are bent on your own ruin, be it so. We know not the way to the Gorgon; but we will ask the giant Atlas, above upon the mountain peak, the brother of our father, the silver Evening Star. He sits aloft and sees across the ocean, and far away into the Unshapen Land.'

So they went up the mountain to Atlas their uncle, and Perseus went up with them. And they found the giant kneeling, as he held the heavens and the earth apart.

They asked him, and he answered mildly, pointing to the seaboard with his mighty hand: 'I can see the Gorgons lying on an island far away, but this youth can never come near them, unless he has the hat of darkness, which whosoever wears cannot be seen.'

Then cried Perseus: 'Where is that hat, that I may find it?'

But the giant smiled. 'No living mortal can find that hat, for it lies in the depths of Hades in the regions of the dead. But my nieces are immortal, and they shall fetch it for you if you will promise me one thing and keep your faith.'

Then Perseus promised; and the giant said: 'When you come back with the head of Medusa, you shall show me the beautiful horror, that I may lose my feeling and my breathing, and become a stone for ever; for it is weary labour for me to hold the heavens and the earth apart.'

Then Perseus promised; and the eldest of the nymphs went down and into a dark cavern among the cliffs out of which came smoke and thunder, for it was one of the mouths of Hell.

And Perseus and the nymphs sat down seven days and waited trembling, till the nymph came up again; and her face was pale and her eyes dazzled with the light, for she had been long in the dreary darkness, but in her hand was the magic hat.

Then all the nymphs kissed Perseus, and wept over him a long while, but he was only impatient to be gone. And at last they put the hat upon his head, and he vanished out of their sight.

But Perseus went on boldly, past many an ugly sight, far away into the heart of the Unshapen Land, beyond the streams of Ocean, to the isles where no ship cruises, where is neither night nor day, where nothing is in its right place and nothing has a name, till he heard the rustle of the Gorgons' wings and saw the glitter of their brazen talons; and then he knew that it was time to halt, lest Medusa should freeze him into stone.

He thought awhile with himself, and remembered Athené's words. He rose aloft into the air and held the mirror of the shield above his head and looked up into it that he might see all that was below him.

And he saw the three Gorgons sleeping, as huge as elephants. He knew that they could not see him because the hat of darkness hid him; and yet he trembled as he sank down near them, so terrible were those brazen claws.

Two of the Gorgons were foul as swine, and lay sleeping heavily as swine sleep, with their mighty wings outspread; but Medusa tossed to and fro restlessly, and as she tossed Perseus pitied her, she looked so fair and said. Her plumage was like the rainbow, and her face was like the face of a nymph; only her eyebrows were knit and her lips clenched, with everlasting care and pain, and her long neck gleamed so white in the mirror that Perseus had not the heart to strike, and said: 'Ah, that it had been either of her sisters!'

But as he looked, from among her tresses the vipers' heads awoke and peeped up with their bright dry eyes and showed their fangs and hissed. And Medusa, as she tossed, threw back her wings and showed her brazen claws; and Perseus saw that, for all her beauty, she was as foul and venomous as the rest.

Then he came down and stepped to her boldly, and looked steadfastly on his mirror, and struck with Herpé stoutly once. And he did not need to strike again.

Then he wrapped the head in the goatskin, turning away his eyes, and sprang into the air aloft, faster than he ever sprang before.

For Medusa's wings and talons rattled as she sank dead upon the rocks, and her two foul sisters woke and saw her lying dead.

Into the air they sprang yelling and looked for him who had done the deed. Thrice they swung round and round, like hawks who beat for a partridge; and thrice they snuffed round and round, like hounds who draw upon a deer. At last they struck upon the scent of the blood, and they checked for a moment to make sure; and then on they rushed with a fearful howl, while the wind rattled hoarse in their wings.

On they rushed, sweeping and flapping like eagles after a hare; and Perseus' blood ran cold, for all his courage, as he saw them come howling on his track; and he cried: 'Bear me well now, brave sandals, for the hounds of Death are at my heels!'

And well the brave sandals bore him, aloft through cloud and sunshine, across the shoreless sea; and fast followed the hounds of Death, as the roar of their wings came down the wind. But the roar came down fainter and fainter, and the howl of their voices died away; for the sandals were too swift, even for Gorgons, and by nightfall they were far behind, two black specks in the southern sky, till the sun sank and he saw them no more.

Then he came again to Atlas and the garden of the nymphs; and when the giant heard him coming, he groaned and said: 'Fulfil thy promise to me.' Then Perseus held up to him the Gorgon's head, and he had rest from all his toil, for he became a crag of stone, which sleeps for ever far above the clouds.

Then he thanked the nymphs, and asked them. 'By what road shall I go homeward again, for I wandered far round in coming hither?'

And they wept and cried: 'Go home no more, but stay and play with us, the lonely maidens, who dwell for ever far away from gods and men.'

But he refused, and they told him his road, and said: 'Take with you this magic fruit, which, if you eat once, you will not

hunger for seven days. For you must go eastward and eastward ever, over the doleful Libyan shore, which Poseidon
gave to Father Zeus, when he burst open the Bosphorus and the
Hellespont, and drowned the fair Lectonian land. And Zeus
took that land in exchange—a fair bargain, much bad ground
for a little good—and to this day it lies waste and desert, with
shingle and rock and sand.'

Then they kissed Perseus and wept over him, and he leapt
down the mountain and went on, lessening and lessening like a
seagull, away and out to sea.

PART IV

How Perseus Came to the Aethiops

So Perseus flitted onward to the north-east, over many a
league of sea, till he came to the rolling sand-hills and the
dreary Libyan shore.

And he flitted on across the desert: over rock ledges and

banks of shingle and level wastes of sand, and shell-drifts bleaching in the sunshine and the skeletons of great sea-monsters and dead bones of ancient giants, strewn up and down upon the old sea-floor. And as he went the blood drops fell to the earth from the Gorgon's head, and became poisonous asps and adders, which breed in the desert to this day.

Over the sands he went—he never knew how far or how long—feeding on the fruit which the nymphs had given him, till he saw the hills of the Psylli, and the dwarfs who fought with cranes. Their spears were of reeds and rushes, and their houses of the egg-shells of the cranes; and Perseus laughed, and went his way to the north-east, hoping all day long to see the blue Mediterranean sparkling, that he might fly across it to his home.

But now came down a mighty wind, and swept him back southward toward the desert. All day long he strove against it; but even the winged sandals could not prevail. So he was forced to float down the wind all night; and when the morning dawned there was nothing to be seen, save the same old hateful waste of sand.

And out of the north the sandstorms rushed upon him, blood-red pillars and wreaths, blotting out the noonday sun; and Perseus fled before them, lest he should be choked by the burning dust. At last the gale fell calm, and he tried to go northward again; but again came down the sandstorms, and swept him back into the waste, and then all was calm and cloudless as before. Seven days he strove against the storms, and seven days he was driven back, till he was spent with thirst and hunger, and his tongue clove to the roof of his mouth. Here and there he fancied that he saw a fair lake, and the sunbeams shining on the water; but when he came to it it vanished at his feet, and there was nought but burning sand. And if he had not been of the race of the Immortals, he would have perished in the waste; but his life was strong within him, because it was more than man's.

Then he cried to Athené, and said:

'Oh, fair and pure, if thou hearest me, wilt thou leave me here to die of drought? I have brought thee the Gorgon's head at thy bidding, and hitherto thou hast prospered my journey; dost thou desert me at the last? Else why will not these immortal sandals prevail, even against the desert storms? Shall I never see my mother more, and the blue ripple round Seriphos, and the sunny hills of Hellas?'

So he prayed; and after he had prayed there was a great silence.

The heaven was still above his head and the sand was still beneath his feet, and Perseus looked up, but there was nothing but the blinding sun in the blinding blue, and round him, but there was nothing but the blinding sand.

And Perseus stood still awhile, and waited, and said: 'Surely I am not here without the will of the Immortals, for Athené will not lie. Were not these sandals to lead me in the right road? Then the road in which I have tried to go must be a wrong road.'

Then suddenly his ears were opened, and he heard the sound of running water.

And at that his heart was lifted up, though he scarcely dare believe his ears; and weary as he was he hurried forward, though he could scarcely stand upright; and within a bowshot of him was a glen in the sand and marble rocks and date trees and a lawn of gay green grass. And through the lawn a stream-let sparkled and wandered out beyond the trees, and vanished in the sand.

The water trickled among the rocks, and a pleasant breeze rustled in the dry date branches; and Perseus laughed for joy and leapt down the cliff and drank of the cool water and ate of the dates and slept upon the turf and leapt up and went forward again, but not toward the north this time. For he said: 'Surely Athené hath sent me hither, and will not have me go homeward yet. What if there be another noble deed to be done before I see the sunny hills of Hellas?'

So he went east, and east for ever, by fresh oases and foun-tains, date palms and lawns of grass, till he saw before him a mighty mountain wall, all rose-red in the setting sun.

Then he towered in the air like an eagle, for his limbs were strong again; and he flew all night across the mountain till the day began to dawn and rosy-fingered Eos came blushing up the sky. And then, behold, beneath him was the long green garden of Egypt and the shining stream of Nile.

And he saw cities walled up to heaven, and temples and obelisks and pyramids and giant gods of stone. And he came down amid fields of barley and flax and millet and clambering gourds, and saw the people coming out of the gates of a great city and setting to work, each in his place, among the water-courses, parting the streams among the plants cunningly with their feet, according to the wisdom of the Egyptians. But when they saw him they all stopped their work and gathered round him and cried:

'Who art thou, fair youth? And what bearest thou beneath thy goatskin there? Surely thou art one of the Immortals, for thy skin is white like ivory and ours is red like clay. Thy hair is like threads of gold and ours is black and curled. Surely thou art one of the Immortals!' And they would have worshipped him then and there, but Perseus said:

'I am not one of the Immortals, but I am a hero of the Hellenes. And I have slain the Gorgon in the wilderness, and bear her head with me. Give me food therefore that I may go forward and finish my work.'

Then they gave him food and fruit and wine, but they would not let him go. And when the news came into the city that the Gorgon was slain, the priests came out to meet him, and the maidens, with songs and dances and timbrels and harps; and they would have brought him to their temple and to their king, but Perseus put on the hat of darkness, and vanished away out of their sight.

Therefore the Egyptians looked long for his return, but in vain, and worshipped him as a hero, and made a statue of him in Chemmis, which stood for many a hundred years. And they said that he appeared to them at times, with sandals a cubit long, and that whenever he appeared the season was fruitful and the Nile rose high that year.

Then Perseus went to the eastward, along the Red Sea shore; and then, because he was afraid to go into the Arabian deserts, he turned northward once more, and this time no storm hindered him.

He went past the Isthmus and Mount Casius and the vast Serbonian bog and up the shore of Palestine, where the dark-faced Aethiops dwelt.

He flew on past pleasant hills and valleys, like Argos itself, or Lacedaemon, or the fair vale of Tempe. But the lowlands were all drowned by floods, and the highlands blasted by fire, and the hills heaved like a bubbling cauldron before the wrath of King Poseidon, the shaker of the earth.

And Perseus feared to go inland, but flew along the shore above the sea. And he went on all the day, and the sky was black with smoke; and he went on all the night, and the sky was red with flame.

And at the dawn of day he looked toward the cliffs, and at the water's edge, under a black rock, he saw a white image stand.

'This', thought he, 'must surely be the statue of some sea-god; I will go near and see what kind of gods these barbarians worship.'

So he came near; but when he came it was no statue, but a maiden of flesh and blood, for he could see her tresses streaming in the breeze. And as he came closer still he could see how she shrank and shivered when the waves sprinkled her with cold salt spray. Her arms were spread above her head, and fastened to the rock with chains of brass; and her head drooped on her bosom, either with sleep or weariness or grief. But now and then she looked up and wailed and called her mother; yet she did not see Perseus, for the cap of darkness was on his head.

Full of pity and indignation, Perseus drew near and looked upon the maid. Her cheeks were darker than his were, and her hair was blue-black like a hyacinth; but Perseus thought: 'I have never seen so beautiful a maiden, no, not in all our isles. Surely she is a king's daughter. Do barbarians treat their king's daughters thus? She is too fair at least to have done any wrong. I will speak to her.'

And lifting the hat from his head he flashed into her sight.

She shrieked with terror and tried to hide her face with her hair, for she could not with her hands; but Perseus cried:

'Do not fear me, fair one; I am a Hellene, and no barbarian. What cruel men have bound you? But first I will set you free.'

And he tore at the fetters, but they were too strong for him, while the maiden cried:

'Touch me not; I am accursed, devoted as a victim to the sea-gods. They will slay you if you dare to set me free.'

'Let them try,' said Perseus, and drawing Herpé from his thigh, he cut through the brass as if it had been flax.

'Now', he said, 'you belong to me and not to these sea-gods, whosoever they may be!' But she only called the more on her mother.

'Why call on your mother? She can be no mother to have left you here. If a bird is dropped out of the nest, it belongs to the man who picks it up. If a jewel is cast by the wayside, it is his who dare win it and wear it as I will win you and will wear you. I know now why Pallas Athené sent me hither. She sent me to gain a prize worth all my toil and more.'

And he clasped her in his arms and cried: 'Where are these sea-gods, cruel and unjust, who doom fair maids to death? I carry the weapons of Immortals. Let them measure their strength against mine! But tell me, maiden, who you are and what dark fate brought you here.'

And she answered, weeping:

'I am the daughter of Cepheus, King of Iopa, and my mother is Cassiopoeia of the beautiful tresses, and they called me Andromeda, as long as life was mine. And I stand bound here, hapless that I am, for the sea-monster's food, to atone for my mother's sin. For she boasted of me once that I was fairer than

Atergatis, Queen of the Fishes; so she in her wrath sent the sea-floods. And her brother the Fire King sent the earthquakes, and wasted all the land, and after the floods a monster bred of the slime, who devours all living things. And now he must devour me, guiltless though I am—me, who never harmed a living thing, nor saw a fish upon the shore but I gave it life and threw it back into the sea, for in our land we eat no fish for fear of Atergatis their queen. Yet the priests say that nothing but my blood can atone for a sin which I never committed.'

But Perseus laughed, and said: 'A sea-monster? I have fought with worse than him: I would have faced Immortals for your sake; how much more a beast of the sea?'

Then Andromeda looked up at him, and new hope was kindled in her breast, so proud and fair did he stand, with one hand round her, and in the other the glittering sword. But she only sighed and wept the more and cried:

'Why will you die, young as you are? Is there not death and sorrow enough in the world already? It is noble for me to die, that I may save the lives of a whole people; but you, better than them all, why should I slay you too? Go you your way; I must go mine.'

But Perseus cried: 'Not so; for the lords of Olympus, whom I serve, are the friends of the heroes and help them on to noble deeds. Led by them I slew the Gorgon, the beautiful horror, and not without them do I come hither, to slay this monster with that same Gorgon's head. Yet hide your eyes when I leave you, lest the sight of it freeze you too to stone.'

But the maiden answered nothing, for she could not believe his words. And then, suddenly looking up, she pointed to the sea, and shrieked:

'There he comes, with the sunrise, as they promised. I must die now. How shall I endure it? Oh, go! Is it not dreadful enough to be torn piecemeal, without having you to look on?' And she tried to thrust him away.

But he said: 'I go; yet promise me one thing ere I go: that if I slay this beast you will be my wife, and come back with me to my kingdom in fruitful Argos, for I am a king's heir. Promise me, and seal it with a kiss.'

Then she lifted up her face and kissed him, and Perseus laughed for joy and flew upward, while Andromeda crouched trembling on the rock, waiting for what might befall.

On came the great sea-monster, coasting along like a huge black galley, lazily breasting the ripple and stopping at times by creek or headland to watch for the laughter of girls at their bleaching, or cattle pawing on the sandhills, or boys bathing on the beach. His great sides were fringed with clustering shells and seaweeds, and the water gurgled in and out of his wide jaws as he rolled along, dripping and glistening in the beams of the morning sun.

At last he saw Andromeda, and shot forward to take his prey, while the waves foamed white behind him, and before him the fish fled leaping.

Then down from the height of the air fell Perseus like a shooting star—down to the crests of the waves, while Andromeda hid her face as he shouted. And then there was silence for a while.

At last she looked up trembling and saw Perseus springing toward her, and instead of the monster a long black rock, with the sea rippling quietly round it.

Who then so proud as Perseus, as he leapt back to the rock,

and lifted his fair Andromeda in his arms and flew with her to the cliff-top, as a falcon carries a dove?

Who so proud as Perseus, and who so joyful as all the Aethiop people? For they had stood watching the monster from the cliffs, wailing for the maiden's fate. And already a messenger had gone to Cepheus and Cassiopoeia, where they sat in sackcloth and ashes on the ground in the innermost palace chambers, awaiting their daughter's end. And they came, and all the city with them, to see the wonder, with songs and with dances, with cymbals and harps, and received their daughter back again, as one alive from the dead.

Then Cepheus said: 'Hero of the Hellenes, stay here with me and be my son-in-law, and I will give you the half of my kingdom.'

'I will be your son-in-law,' said Perseus, 'but of your kingdom I will have none, for I long after the pleasant land of Greece, and my mother who waits for me at home.'

Then Cepheus said: 'You must not take my daughter away at once, for she is to us like one alive from the dead. Stay with us here a year, and after that you shall return with honour.' And Perseus consented; but before he went to the palace he bade the people bring stones and wood, and built three altars— one to Athené, one to Hermes and one to Father Zeus—and offered bullocks and rams.

And some said: 'This is a pious man.' Yet the priests said: 'The Sea Queen will be yet more fierce against us, because her monster is slain.' But they were afraid to speak aloud, for they feared the Gorgon's head. So they went up to the palace; and when they came in there stood in the hall Phineus, the brother of Cepheus, chafing like a bear robbed of her whelps, and with him his sons and his servants and many an armed man; and he cried to Cepheus:

'You shall not marry your daughter to this stranger, of whom no one knows even the name. Was not Andromeda betrothed to my son? And now she is safe again, has he not a right to claim her?'

But Perseus laughed and answered: 'If your son is in want of a bride, let him save a maiden for himself. As yet he seems but a helpless bridegroom. He left this one to die, and dead she is to him. I saved her alive, and alive she is to me, but to no one else. Ungrateful man! Have I not saved your land and the lives of your sons and daughters, and will you requite me thus? Go, or it will be worse for you!' But all the men-at-arms drew their swords and rushed on him like wild beasts.

Then he unveiled the Gorgon's head, and said: 'This has delivered my bride from one wild beast: it shall deliver her from many.' And as he spoke Phineus and all his men-at-arms stopped short, and each man stiffened as he stood; and before Perseus had drawn the goatskin over the face again, they were all turned into stone.

Then Perseus bade the people bring levers and roll them out. And what was done with them after that I cannot tell.

So they made a great wedding-feast, which lasted seven whole days, and who so happy as Perseus and Andromeda?

But on the eighth night Perseus dreamed a dream, and he saw standing beside him Pallas Athené, as he had seen her in Seriphos, seven long years before. And she stood and called him by name, and said:

'Perseus, you have played the man, and see, you have your reward. Know now that the gods are just, and help him who helps himself. Now give me here Herpé the sword and the sandals and the hat of darkness, that I may give them back to their owners, but the Gorgon's head you shall keep awhile, for you will need it in your land of Greece. Then you shall lay it up in my temple at Seriphos, that I may wear it on my shield for ever, a terror to the Titans and the monsters and the foes of gods and men. And as for this land, I have appeased the sea and the fire, and there shall be no more floods nor earthquakes. But let the people build altars to Father Zeus and to me, and worship the Immortals, the lords of heaven and earth.'

And Perseus rose to give her the sword and the cap and the sandals, but he woke, and his dream vanished away. And yet it was not altogether a dream, for the goatskin with the head was in its place, but the sword and the cap and the sandals were gone, and Perseus never saw them more.

Then a great awe fell on Perseus. And he went out in the morning to the people and told his dream and bade them build altars to Zeus, the father of gods and men, and to Athené, who gives wisdom to heroes, and fear no more the earthquakes and the floods, but sow and build in peace. And they did so for a while, and prospered. But after Perseus was gone they forgot Zeus and Athené, and worshipped again Atergatis the queen, and the undying fish of the sacred lake, where Deucalion's deluge was swallowed up; and they burnt their children before the Fire King, till Zeus was angry with that foolish people and brought a strange nation against them out of Egypt, who fought against them and wasted them utterly, and dwelt in their cities for many a hundred years.

PART V

How Perseus Came Home Again

AND when a year was ended Perseus hired Phoenicians from Tyre and cut down cedars, and built himself a noble galley, and painted its cheeks with vermilion and pitched its sides with pitch. And in it he put Andromeda and all her dowry of jewels and rich shawls and spices from the East, and great was the weeping when they rowed away. But the remembrance of his brave deed was left behind; and Andromeda's rock was shown at Iopa in Palestine till more than a thousand years were past.

So Perseus and the Phoenicians rowed to the westward across the sea of Crete, till they came to the blue Aegean and the pleasant Isles of Hellas and Seriphos, his ancient home.

Then he left his galley on the beach, and went up as of old, and he embraced his mother and Dictys his good foster-father, and they wept over each other a long while, for it was seven years and more since they had met.

Then Perseus went out, and up to the hall of Polydectes; and underneath the goatskin he bore the Gorgon's head.

And when he came into the hall, Polydectes sat at the table-head, and all his nobles and landowners on either side, each according to his rank, feasting on the fish and the goat's flesh, and drinking the blood-red wine. The harpers harped and the revellers shouted, and the wine-cups rang merrily as they passed from hand to hand, and great was the noise in the hall of Polydectes.

Then Perseus stood upon the threshold and called to the king by name. But none of the guests knew Perseus, for he was changed by his long journey. He had gone out a boy, and he was come home a hero; his eye shone like an eagle's and his beard was like a lion's beard, and he stood up like a wild bull in his pride.

But Polydectes the wicked knew him, and hardened his heart still more; and scornfully he called:

'Ah, foundling! Have you found it more easy to promise than to fulfil?'

'Those whom the gods help fulfil their promises; and those who despise them, reap as they have sown. Behold the Gorgon's head!'

Then Perseus drew back the goatskin, and held aloft the Gorgon's head.

Pale grew Polydectes and his guests as they looked upon that dreadful face. They tried to rise up from their seats: but from their seats they never rose, but stiffened, each man where he sat, into a ring of cold grey stones.

Then Perseus turned and left them, and went down to his galley in the bay. And he gave the kingdom to good Dictys, and sailed away with his mother and his bride.

And Polydectes and his guests sat still, with the wine-cups before them on the board, till the rafters crumbled down above their heads and the walls behind their backs, and the table crumbled down between them, and the grass sprang up about their feet; but Polydectes and his guests sit on the hillside, a ring of grey stones until this day.

But Perseus rowed westward toward Argos, and landed, and went up to the town. And when he came, he found that Acrisius his grandfather had fled. For Proetus his wicked brother had made war against him afresh, and had come across the river from Tiryns and conquered Argos, and Acrisius had fled to Larissa in the country of the wild Pelasgi.

Then Perseus called the Argives together and told them who he was, and all the noble deeds which he had done. And all the nobles and the yeomen made him king, for they saw that he had a royal heart; and they fought with him against Argos, and took it, and killed Proetus, and made the Cyclopes serve them, and build them walls round Argos, like the walls which they had built at Tiryns. And there were great rejoicings in the vale of Argos, because they had got a king from Father Zeus.

But Perseus' heart yearned after his grandfather, and he said: 'Surely he is my flesh and blood, and he will love me now that I am come home with honour; I will go and find him, and bring him home, and we will reign together in peace.'

So Perseus sailed away with his Phoenicians, round Hydrea and Sunium, past Marathon and the Attic shore, and through Euripus, and up the long Euboean sea, till he came to the town of Larissa, where the wild Pelasgi dwelt.

And when he came there all the people were in the fields and there was feasting, and all kinds of games; for Teutamenes their king wished to honour Acrisius, because he was the king of a mighty land.

So Perseus did not tell his name, but went up to the games unknown; for he said: 'If I carry away the prize in the games, my grandfather's heart will be softened toward me.'

So he threw off his helmet and his cuirass and all his clothes, and stood among the youths of Larissa, while all wondered at him, and said: 'Who is this young stranger, who stands like a wild bull in his pride? Surely he is one of the heroes, the sons of the Immortals, from Olympus.'

And when the games began they wondered yet more; for Perseus was the best man of all at running and leaping and wrestling and throwing the javelin; and he won four crowns, and took them, and then he said to himself: 'There is a fifth crown yet to be won: I will win that, and lay them all upon the knees of my grandfather.'

And as he spoke he saw where Acrisius sat, by the side of Teutamenes the king, with his white beard flowing down upon his knees, and his royal staff in his hand; and Perseus wept when he looked at him, for his heart yearned after his kin; and he said. 'Surely he is a kingly old man; yet he need not be ashamed of his grandson.'

Then he took the quoits and hurled them five fathoms beyond all the rest, and the people shouted: 'Farther yet, brave stranger! There has never been such a hurler in this land.'

Then Perseus put out all his strength and hurled. But a gust of wind came from the sea and carried the quoit aside, and far beyond all the rest, and it fell on the foot of Acrisius, and he swooned away with the pain.

Perseus shrieked and ran up to him; but when they lifted the old man up he was dead, for his life was slow and feeble.

Then Perseus rent his clothes and cast dust upon his head and wept a long while for his grandfather. At last he rose and called to all the people aloud, and said:

'The gods are true, and what they have ordained must be. I am Perseus, the grandson of this dead man, the far-famed slayer of the Gorgon.'

Then he told them how the prophecy had declared that he should kill his grandfather, and all the story of his life.

So they made a great mourning for Acrisius and burnt him on a right rich pile, and Perseus went to the temple, and was purified from the guilt of the death, because he had done it unknowingly.

Then he went home to Argos, and reigned there well with fair Andromeda, and they had four sons and three daughters, and died in a good old age.

And when they died, the ancients say, Athené took them up into the sky, with Cepheus and Cassiopoeia. And there on starlight nights you may see them shining still—Cepheus with his kingly crown, and Cassiopoeia in her ivory chair, plaiting her star-spangled tresses, and Perseus with the Gorgon's head, and fair Andromeda beside him, spreading her long white arms across the heaven, as she stood when chained to the stone for the monster. All night long they shine for a beacon to wandering sailors; but all day they feast with the gods, on the still blue peaks of Olympus.

The Argonauts

PART I

How the Centaur Trained the Heroes on Pelion

I HAVE told you of a hero who fought with wild beasts and with wild men; but now I have a tale of heroes who sailed away into a distant land, to win themselves renown for ever, in the adventure of the Golden Fleece.

Whither they sailed, my children, I cannot clearly tell. It all happened long ago; so long that it has all grown dim, like a dream which you dreamt last year. And why they went I cannot tell: some say that it was to win gold. It may be so; but the noblest deeds which have been done on earth have not been done for gold. It was not for the sake of gold that the Lord came down and died, and the Apostles went out to preach the good news in all lands. The Spartans looked for no reward in money when they fought and died at Thermopylae; and

Socrates the wise asked no pay from his countrymen, but lived poor and barefoot all his days, only caring to make men good. And there are heroes in our days also, who do noble deeds, but not for gold. Our discoverers did not go to make themselves rich when they sailed out one after another into the dreary frozen seas; nor did the ladies who went out last year to drudge in the hospitals of the East,[1] making themselves poor, that they might be rich in noble works. And young men, too, whom you know, children, and some of them of your own kin, did they say to themselves, 'How much money shall I earn?' when they went out to the war, leaving wealth and comfort and a pleasant home and all that money can give, to face hunger and thirst and wounds and death, that they might fight for their country and their Queen? No, children, there is a better thing on earth than wealth, a better thing than life itself; and that is to have done something before you die, for which good men may honour you, and God your Father may smile upon your work.

Therefore we will believe—why should we not?—of these same Argonauts of old, that they too were noble men, who planned and did a noble deed; and that therefore their fame has lived and been told in story and in song, mixed up, no doubt, with dreams and fables, and yet true and right at heart. So we will honour these old Argonauts, and listen to their story as it stands; and we will try to be like them, each of us in our place; for each of us has a Golden Fleece to seek and a wild sea to sail over ere we reach it and dragons to fight ere it be ours.

And what was that first Golden Fleece? I do not know, nor care. The old Hellenes said that it hung in Colchis, which we

[1] The Crimean War, 1853–6.

call the Circassian coast, nailed to a beech tree in the war-god's wood; and that it was the fleece of the wondrous ram who bore Phrixus and Helle across the Euxine Sea. For Phrixus and Helle were the children of the cloud-nymphs and of Athamas the Minyan king. And when a famine came upon the land, their cruel stepmother Ino wished to kill them, that her own children might reign, and said that they must be sacrificed on an altar, to turn away the anger of the gods. So the poor children were brought to the altar, and the priest stood ready with his knife, when out of the clouds came the Golden Ram, and took them on his back, and vanished. Then madness came upon that foolish king, Athamas, and ruin upon Ino and her children. For Athamas killed one of them in his fury, and Ino fled from him with the other in her arms and leaped from a cliff into the sea and was changed into a dolphin, such as you have seen, which wanders over the waves for ever sighing, with its little one clasped to its breast.

But the people drove out King Athamas, because he had killed his child; and he roamed about in his misery till he came to the Oracle in Delphi. And the Oracle told him that he must wander for his sin, till the wild beasts should feast him as their guest. So he went on in hunger and sorrow for many a weary day, till he saw a pack of wolves. The wolves were tearing a sheep; but when they saw Athamas they fled, and left the sheep for him, and he ate of it. And then he knew that the oracle was fulfilled at last. So he wandered no more, but settled and built a town and became a king again.

But the ram carried the two children far away over land and sea, till he came to the Thracian Chersonese, and there Helle fell into the sea. So those narrow straits are called

'Hellespont' after her; and they bear that name until this day.

Then the ram flew on with Phrixus to the north-east across the sea which we call the Black Sea now; but the Hellenes call it Euxine. And at last, they say, he stopped at Colchis on the steep Circassian coast; and there Phrixus married Chalciope, the daughter of Aietes the king, and offered the ram in sacrifice; and Aietes nailed the ram's fleece to a beech, in the grove of Ares the war-god.

And after a while Phrixus died and was buried, but his spirit had no rest; for he was buried far from his native land, and the pleasant hills of Hellas. So he came in dreams to the heroes of the Minyae and called sadly by their beds: 'Come and set my spirit free, that I may go home to my fathers and to my kinsfolk and the pleasant Minyan land.'

And they asked: 'How shall we set your spirit free?'

'You must sail over the sea to Colchis and bring home the golden fleece; and then my spirit will come back with it and I shall sleep with my fathers and have rest.'

He came thus and called to them often; but when they woke they looked at each other, and said: 'Who dare sail to Colchis, or bring home the golden fleece?' And in all the country none was brave enough to try it; for the man and the time were not come.

Phrixus had a cousin called Aeson, who was king in Iolcos by the sea. There he ruled over the rich Minyan heroes, as Athamas his uncle ruled in Boeotia; and like Athamas he was an unhappy man. For he had a stepbrother named Pelias, of whom some said that he was a nymph's son, and there were dark and sad tales about his birth. When he was a babe he was cast out

on the mountains, and a wild mare came by and kicked him.
But a passing shepherd found the baby, with its face all
blackened by the blow, and took him home and called him
Pelias, because his face was bruised and black. And he grew up
fierce and lawless, and did many a fearful deed. And at last he
drove out Aeson his stepbrother, and then his own brother
Neleus, and took the kingdom to himself, and ruled over the
rich Minyan heroes, in Iolcos by the sea.

And Aeson, when he was driven out, went sadly out of the
town, leading his little son by the hand; and he said to himself:
'I must hide the child in the mountains, or Pelias will surely
kill him, because he is the heir.'

So he went up from the sea across the valley, through the
vineyards and the olive groves, and across the torrent of
Anauros, toward Pelion the ancient mountain, whose brows are
white with snow.

He went up and up into the mountain, over marsh and crag
and down, till the boy was tired and footsore, and Aeson had to
bear him in his arms, till he came to the mouth of a lonely cave
at the foot of a mighty cliff.

Above the cliff the snow wreaths hung, dripping and crack-
ing in the sun; but at its foot around the cave's mouth grew all
fair flowers and herbs, as if in a garden, ranged in order, each
sort by itself. There they grew gaily in the sunshine and the
spray of the torrent from above, while from the cave came the
sound of music and a man's voice singing to the harp.

Then Aeson put down the lad and whispered:

'Fear not, but go in, and whomsoever you shall find, lay
your hands upon his knees and say: "In the name of Zeus, the
father of gods and men, I am your guest from this day forth."'

Then the lad went in without trembling, for he too was a hero's son; but when he was within, he stopped in wonder to listen to that magic song.

And there he saw the singer lying upon bearskins and fragrant boughs—Cheiron, the ancient centaur, the wisest of all things beneath the sky. Down to the waist he was a man, but

below he was a noble horse; his white hair rolled down over his broad shoulders, and his white beard over his broad brown chest, and his eyes were wise and mild, and his forehead like a mountain wall.

And in his hands he held a harp of gold and struck it with a golden key; and as he struck he sang till his eyes glittered and filled all the cave with light.

And he sang of the birth of time, and of the heavens and the dancing stars, and of the ocean and the ether and the fire and the shaping of the wondrous earth. And he sang of the treasures of the hills and the hidden jewels of the mine and the veins of fire and metal, and the virtues of all healing herbs, and of the speech of birds, and of prophecy and of hidden things to come.

Then he sang of health and strength and manhood and a valiant heart, and of music and hunting and wrestling, and all the games which heroes love, and of travel, and wars and sieges and a noble death in fight, and then he sang of peace and plenty, and of equal justice in the land, and as he sang the boy listened wide-eyed and he forgot his errand in the song.

And at the last old Cheiron was silent, and called the lad with a soft voice.

And the lad ran trembling to him, and would have laid his hands upon his knees; but Cheiron smiled and said: 'Call hither your father Aeson, for I know you and all that has befallen, and saw you both afar in the valley, even before you left the town.'

Then Aeson came in sadly and Cheiron asked him: 'Why camest you not yourself to me, Aeson the Aeolid?'

And Aeson said:

'I thought, Cheiron will pity the lad if he sees him come alone; and I wished to try whether he was fearless and dare venture like a hero's son. But now I entreat you by Father Zeus, let the boy be your guest till better times, and train him among the sons of the heroes, that he may avenge his father's house.'

Then Cheiron smiled and drew the lad to him, and laid his hand upon his golden locks, and said: 'Are you afraid of my horse's hoofs, fair boy, or will you be my pupil from this day?'

'I would gladly have horse's hoofs like you, if I could sing such songs as yours.'

And Cheiron laughed, and said: 'Sit here by me till

sundown, when your playfellows will come home, and you shall learn like them to be a king, worthy to rule over gallant men.'

Then he turned to Aeson, and said: 'Go back in peace, and bend before the storm like a prudent man. This boy shall not cross the Anauros again, till he has become a glory to you and to the house of Aeolus.'

And Aeson wept over his son and went away; but the boy did not weep, so full was his fancy of that strange cave and the centaur and his song and the playfellows whom he was to see.

Then Cheiron put the lyre into his hands, and taught him how to play it, till the sun sank low behind the cliff and a shout was heard outside.

And then in came the sons of the heroes—Aeneas and Heracles and Peleus and many another mighty name.

And great Cheiron leapt up joyfully and his hoofs made the cave resound, as they shouted: 'Come out, Father Cheiron! Come out and see our game.' And one cried, 'I have killed two deer,' and another, 'I took a wild cat among the crags'. And Heracles dragged a wild goat after him by its horns, for he was as huge as a mountain crag, and Coeneus carried a bear cub under each arm and laughed when they scratched and bit, for neither tooth nor steel could wound him.

And Cheiron praised them all, each according to his deserts.

Only one walked apart and silent: Asclepius, the too-wise child, with his bosom full of herbs and flowers, and round his wrist a spotted snake; he came with downcast eyes to Cheiron, and whispered how he had watched the snake cast its old skin and grow young again before his eyes, and how he had gone down into a village in the vale and cured a dying man with a herb which he had seen a sick goat eat.

And Cheiron smiled, and said: 'To each Athené and Apollo give some gift, and each is worthy in his place; but to this child they have given an honour beyond all honours, to cure while others kill.'

Then the lads brought in wood, and split it and lighted a blazing fire, and others skinned the deer and quartered them and set them to roast before the fire; and while the venison was cooking they bathed in the snow torrent, and dashed away the dust and sweat.

And then all ate till they could eat no more (for they had tasted nothing since the dawn), and drank of the clear spring water, for wine is not fit for growing lads. And when the remnants were put away, they all lay down upon the skins and leaves about the fire, and each took the lyre in turn, and sang and played with all his heart.

And after a while they all went out to a plot of grass at the cave's mouth, and there they boxed and ran and wrestled and laughed till the stones fell from the cliffs.

Then Cheiron took his lyre, and all the lads joined hands; and as he played they danced to his measure, in and out, and round and round. There they danced hand in hand, till the night fell over land and sea, while the black glen shone with their broad white limbs and the gleam of their golden hair.

And the lad danced with them delighted, and then slept a wholesome sleep upon fragrant leaves of bay and myrtle and marjoram and flowers of thyme, and rose at the dawn and bathed in the torrent and became a schoolfellow to the heroes' sons, and forgot Iolcos and his father and all his former life. But he grew strong and brave and cunning, upon the pleasant downs of Pelion, in the keen, hungry mountain air. And he

learnt to wrestle and to box and to hunt and to play upon the
harp; and next he learnt to ride, for old Cheiron used to mount
him on his back; and he learnt the virtues of all herbs, and how
to cure all wounds; and Cheiron called him Jason the healer,
and that is his name until this day.

PART II

How Jason Lost his Sandal in Anauros

AND ten years came and went, and Jason was grown to
be a mighty man. Some of his fellows were gone and
some were growing up by his side. Asclepius was
gone into Peloponnese to work his wondrous cures on men;
and some say he used to raise the dead to life. And Heracles
was gone to Thebes to fulfil those famous labours which have
become a proverb among men. And Peleus had married a sea-
nymph, and his wedding is famous to this day. And Aeneas

was gone home to Troy, and many a noble tale you will read of him, and of all the other gallant heroes, the scholars of Cheiron the just. And it happened on a day that Jason stood on the mountain, and looked north and south and east and west; and Cheiron stood by him and watched him, for he knew that the time was come.

And Jason looked and saw the plains of Thessaly, where the Lapithai breed their horses, and the lake of Boibé, and the stream which runs northward to Peneus and Tempe; and he looked north, and saw the mountain wall which guards the Magnesian shore, Olympus, the seat of the Immortals, and Ossa, and Pelion where he stood. Then he looked east and saw the bright blue sea, which stretched away for ever toward the dawn. Then he looked south and saw a pleasant land with white-walled towns and farms, nestling along the shore of a land-locked bay, while the smoke rose blue among the trees; and he knew it for the bay of Pagasai, and the rich lowlands of Haemonia, and Iolcos by the sea.

Then he sighed, and asked: 'Is it true what the heroes tell me—that I am heir of that fair land?'

'And what good would it be to you, Jason, if you were heir of that fair land?'

'I would take it and keep it.'

'A strong man has taken it and kept it long. Are you stronger than Pelias the terrible?'

'I can try my strength with his,' said Jason; but Cheiron sighed, and said:

'You have many a danger to go through before you rule in Iolcos by the sea, many a danger and many a woe, and strange troubles in strange lands, such as man never saw before.'

'The happier I', said Jason, 'to see what man never saw before.'

And Cheiron sighed again, and said: 'The eaglet must leave the nest when it is fledged. Will you go to Iolcos by the sea? Then promise me two things before you go.'

Jason promised, and Cheiron answered: 'Speak harshly to no soul whom you may meet, and stand by the word which you shall speak.'

Jason wondered why Cheiron asked this of him, but he knew that the Centaur was a prophet, and saw things long before they came. So he promised, and leapt down the mountain, to take his fortune like a man.

He went down through the arbutus thickets, and across the downs of thyme, till he came to the vineyard walls and the pomegranates and the olives in the glen; and among the olives roared Anauros, all foaming with a summer flood.

And on the bank of Anauros sat a woman, all wrinkled, grey and old; her head shook palsied on her breast, and her hands shook palsied on her knees; and when she saw Jason she spoke whining: 'Who will carry me across the flood?'

Jason was bold and hasty, and was just going to leap into the flood; and yet he thought twice before he leapt, so loud roared the torrent down, all brown from the mountain rains, and silver-veined with melting snow; while underneath he could hear the boulders rumbling like the tramp of horsemen or the roll of wheels, as they ground along the narrow channel, and shook the rocks on which he stood.

But the old woman whined all the more: 'I am weak and old, fair youth. For Hera's sake, carry me over the torrent.'

And Jason was going to answer her scornfully, when Cheiron's words came to his mind.

So he said: 'For Hera's sake, the Queen of the Immortals on Olympus, I will carry you over the torrent, unless we both are drowned midway.'

Then the old dame leapt upon his back as nimbly as a goat, and Jason staggered in, wondering; and the first step was up to his knees.

The first step was up to his knees and the second step was up to his waist; and the stones rolled about his feet, and his feet slipped about the stones, so he went on staggering and panting, while the old woman cried from off his back:

'Fool, you have wet my mantle! Do you make game of poor old souls like me?'

Jason had half a mind to drop her and let her get through the torrent by herself; but Cheiron's words were in his mind, and he said only: 'Patience, mother; the best horse may stumble some day.'

At last he staggered to the shore and set her down upon the bank, and a strong man he needed to have been, or that wild water he never would have crossed.

He lay panting awhile upon the bank, and then leapt up to go upon his journey, but he cast one look at the old woman, for he thought: 'She should thank me once at least.'

And as he looked, she grew fairer than all women, and taller than all men on earth, and her garments shone like the summer sea, and her jewels like the stars of heaven; and over her forehead was a veil, woven of the golden clouds of sunset, and through the veil she looked down on him with great soft heifer's eyes, with great eyes, mild and awful, which filled all the glen with light.

And Jason fell upon his knees, and hid his face between his hands.

And she spoke: 'I am the Queen of Olympus, Hera the wife of Zeus. As thou hast done to me, so will I do to thee. Call on me in the hour of need, and try if the Immortals can forget.'

And when Jason looked up, she rose from off the earth like a pillar of tall white cloud and floated away across the mountain peaks towards Olympus the holy hill.

Then a great fear fell on Jason: but after a while he grew light of heart, and he blessed old Cheiron, and said: 'Surely the Centaur is a prophet, and guessed what would come to pass, when he bade me speak harshly to no soul whom I might meet.'

Then he went down toward Iolcos; and as he walked he found that he had lost one of his sandals in the flood.

And as he went through the streets, the people came out to look at him, so tall and fair was he. But some of the elders whispered together, and at last one of them stopped Jason, and called on him: 'Fair lad, who are you, and whence come you? And what is your errand in the town?'

'My name, good father, is Jason, and I come from Pelion up above; and my errand is to Pelias your king; tell me then where his palace is.'

But the old man started and grew pale, and said: 'Do you not know the oracle, my son, that you go so boldly through the town with but one sandal on?'

'I am a stranger here and know of no oracle; but what of my one sandal? I lost the other in Anauros, while I was struggling with the flood.'

Then the old man looked back to his companions, and one
sighed and another smiled. At last he said: 'I will tell you, lest
you rush upon your ruin unawares. The Oracle in Delphi has
said that a man wearing one sandal should take the kingdom
from Pelias, and keep it for himself. Therefore beware how you
go up to his palace, for he is the fiercest and most cunning of
all kings.'

Then Jason laughed a great laugh like a war-horse in his
pride. 'Good news, good father, both for you and me. For that
very end I came into the town.'

Then he strode on toward the palace of Pelias, while all the
people wondered at his bearing.

And he stood in the doorway and cried: 'Come out,
come out, Pelias the valiant, and fight for your kingdom like
a man.'

Pelias came out wondering, and, 'Who are you, bold youth?'
he cried.

'I am Jason, the son of Aeson, the heir of all this land.'

Then Pelias lifted up his hands and eyes, and wept, or

seemed to weep, and blessed the heavens which had brought his nephew to him, never to leave him more. 'For', said he, 'I have but three daughters, and no son to be my heir. You shall be my heir then, and rule the kingdom after me, and marry whichsoever of my daughters you shall choose. Though a sad kingdom you will find it, and whosoever rules it a miserable man. But come in, come in and feast.'

So he drew Jason in, whether he would or not, and spoke to him so lovingly and feasted him so well, that Jason's anger passed, and after supper his three cousins came into the hall, and Jason thought that he should like well enough to have one of them for his wife.

But at last he said to Pelias: 'Why do you look so sad, my uncle? And what did you mean just now when you said that this was a doleful kingdom and its ruler a miserable man?'

Then Pelias sighed heavily again and again and again, like a man who had to tell some dreadful story, and was afraid to begin; but at last:

'For seven long years and more have I never known a quiet night, and no more will he who comes after me, till the golden fleece be brought home.'

Then he told Jason the story of Phrixus, and of the golden fleece; and told him, too—which was a lie—that Phrixus' spirit tormented him, calling to him day and night. And his daughters came, and told the same tale—for their father had taught them their parts—and wept, and said: 'Oh, who will bring home the golden fleece, that our uncle's spirit may rest, and that we may have rest also, whom he never lets sleep in peace?'

Jason sat awhile, sad and silent; for he had often heard of

that golden fleece, but he looked on it as a thing hopeless and impossible for any mortal man to win.

But when Pelias saw him silent, he began to talk of other things, and courted Jason more and more, speaking to him as if he was certain to be his heir and asking his advice about the kingdom; till Jason, who was young and simple, could not help saying to himself: 'Surely he is not the dark man whom people call him. Yet why did he drive my father out?' And he asked Pelias boldly: 'Men say that you are terrible, and a man of blood; but I find you a kind and hospitable man, and as you are to me, so will I be to you. Yet why did you drive my father out?'

Pelias smiled, and sighed. 'Men have slandered me in that, as in all things. Your father was growing old and weary, and he gave the kingdom up to me of his own will. You shall see him tomorrow and ask him, and he will tell you the same.'

Jason's heart leapt in him when he heard that he was to see his father, and he believed all that Pelias said, forgetting that his father might not dare to tell the truth.

'One thing more there is,' said Pelias, 'on which I need your advice; for though you are young I see in you a wisdom beyond your years. There is one neighbour of mine, whom I dread more than all men on earth. I am stronger than he now and can command him, but I know that if he stay among us, he will work my ruin in the end. Can you give me a plan, Jason, by which I can rid myself of that man?'

After a while Jason answered, half laughing: 'Were I you, I would send him to fetch that same golden fleece; for if he once set forth after it you would never be troubled with him more.'

And at that a bitter smile came across Pelias' lips, and a flash of wicked joy into his eyes; and Jason saw it and started; and over his mind came the warning of the old man, and his own one sandal, and the oracle, and he saw that he was taken in a trap.

But Pelias only answered gently: 'My son, he shall be sent forthwith.'

'You mean me?' cried Jason, starting up, 'because I came here with one sandal?' And he lifted his fist angrily, while Pelias stood up to him like a wolf at bay; and which of the two was the stronger and fiercer it would be hard to tell.

But after a moment Pelias spoke gently: 'Why then so rash, my son? You, and not I, have said what is said; why blame me for what I have not done? Had you bid me love the man of whom I spoke and make him my son-in-law and heir, I would have obeyed you; and what if I obey you now, and send the man to win himself immortal fame? I have not harmed you or him. One thing at least I know, that he will go, and that gladly; for he has a hero's heart within him, loving glory, and scorning to break the word which he has given.'

Jason saw that he was entrapped; but his second promise to Cheiron came into his mind, and he thought: 'What if the Centaur were a prophet in that also, and meant that I should win the fleece!' Then he cried aloud:

'You have well spoken, cunning uncle of mine! I love glory, and I dare keep to my word. I will go and fetch this golden fleece. Promise me but this in return, and keep your word as I keep mine. Treat my father lovingly while I am gone, for the sake of the all-seeing Zeus, and give me up the kingdom for my own on the day that I bring back the golden fleece.'

See page 44

THEN PERSEUS PUT OUT ALL HIS STRENGTH AND HURLED

Then Pelias looked at him and almost loved him, in the midst of all his hate, and said: 'I promise, and I will perform. It will be no shame to give up my kingdom to the man who wins that fleece.'

Then they swore a great oath between them, and afterwards both went in, and lay down to sleep.

But Jason could not sleep for thinking of his mighty oath, and how he was to fulfil it, all alone, and without wealth or friends. So he tossed a long time upon his bed and thought of this plan and of that, and sometimes Phrixus seemed to call him, in a thin voice, faint and low, as if it came from far across the sea: 'Let me come home to my fathers and have rest.' And sometimes he seemed to see the eyes of Hera, and to hear her words again: 'Call on me in the hour of need, and see if the Immortals can forget.'

And on the morrow he went to Pelias, and said: 'Give me a victim, that I may sacrifice to Hera.' So he went up and offered his sacrifice, and as he stood by the altar Hera sent a thought into his mind; and he went back to Pelias, and said:

'If you are indeed in earnest, give me two heralds, that they may go round to all the princes of the Minyae, who were pupils of the Centaur with me, that we may fit out a ship together and take what shall befall.'

At that Pelias praised his wisdom and hastened to send the heralds out; for he said in his heart: 'Let all the princes go with him, and like him never return; for so I shall be lord of all the Minyae, and the greatest king in Hellas.'

PART III

How They Built the Ship *ARGO* in Iolcos

So the heralds went out, and cried to all the heroes of the Minyae: 'Who dare come to the adventure of the golden fleece?'

And Hera stirred the hearts of all the princes, and they came from all their valleys to the yellow sands of Pagasai. And first came Heracles the mighty, with his lion's skin and club, and behind him Hylas his young squire, who bore his arrows and his bow, and Tiphys, the skilful steersman, and Butes, the fairest of all men, and Castor and Polydeuces the twins, the sons of the magic swan, and Caeneus, the strongest of mortals, whom the Centaurs tried in vain to kill, and overwhelmed him with trunks of pine trees, but even so he would not die. And thither came Zetes and Calais, the winged sons of the North Wind, and Peleus, the father of Achilles, whose bride was silver-footed Thetis, the goddess of the sea. And thither came Telamon and Oileus, the fathers of the two Aiantes, who fought upon the plans of Troy, and Mopsus, the wise soothsayer, who knew the speech of birds, and Idmon, to whom Phoebus gave a tongue to prophesy of things to come, and Ancaios, who could read the stars, and knew all the circles of the heavens, and Argus, the famed shipbuilder, and many a hero more, in helmets of brass and gold with tall dyed horse-hair crests, and embroidered shirts of linen beneath their coats of mail, and greaves of polished tin to guard their knees in fight, with each man his shield upon his shoulder, of many a fold of tough bull's hide, and his sword of tempered bronze in his silver-studded belt, and in his right hand a pair of lances, of the heavy white ash-staves.

So they came down to Iolcos, and all the city came out to meet them, and were never tired with looking at their height and their beauty and their gallant bearing, and the glitter of their inlaid arms. And some said: 'Never was such a gathering of the heroes since the Hellenes conquered the land.' But the women sighed over them, and whispered: 'Alas! they are all going to their death!'

Then they felled the pines on Pelion and shaped them with the axe, and Argus taught them to build a galley, the first long ship which ever sailed the seas. They pierced her for fifty oars —an oar for each hero of the crew—and pitched her with coal-black pitch, and painted her bows with vermilion; and they named her *Argo* after Argus, and worked at her all day long. And at night Pelias feasted them like a king, and they slept in his palace porch.

But Jason went away to the northward, and into the land of Thrace, till he found Orpheus the prince of minstrels, where he dwelt in his cave under Rhodope, among the savage Cicon tribes. And he asked him: 'Will you leave your mountains, Orpheus, my fellow scholar in old times, and cross Strymon once more with me to sail with the heroes of the Minyae, and bring home the golden fleece, and charm for us all men and all monsters with your magic harp and song?'

Then Orpheus sighed: 'Have I not had enough of toil and of weary wandering far and wide since I lived in Cheiron's cave, above Iolcos by the sea? In vain is the skill and the voice which my goddess mother gave me; in vain have I sung and laboured; in vain I went down to the dead, and charmed all the kings of Hades, to win back Eurydice my bride. For I won her, my beloved, and lost her again the same day, and wandered away in my madness, even to Egypt and the Libyan sands, and the isles of all the seas, driven on by the terribly gadfly, while I charmed in vain the hearts of men, and the savage forest beasts, and the trees, and the lifeless stones, with my magic harp and song, giving rest, but finding none. But at last Calliope my mother delivered me, and brought me home in peace; and I dwell here in the cave alone, among the savage Cicon tribes, softening their wild hearts with music and the gentle laws of Zeus. And now I must go out again to the ends of all the earth, far away into the misty darkness, to the last wave of the Eastern Sea. But what is doomed must be, and a friend's demand obeyed; for prayers are the daughters of Zeus, and who honours them honours him.'

Then Orpheus rose up sighing, and took his harp and went over Strymon. And he led Jason to the south-west, up the banks of Haliacmon and over the spurs of Pindus, to Dodona the town of Zeus, where it stood by the side of the sacred lake and the fountain which breathed out fire in the darkness of the ancient oakwood beneath the mountain of the hundred springs. And he led him to the holy oak, where the black dove settled in old times, and was changed into the priestess of Zeus, and gave oracles to all nations round. And he bade him cut down a bough, and sacrifice to Hera and to Zeus; and they took the bough and came to Iolcos, and nailed it to the beak-head of the ship.

And at last the ship was finished, and they tried to launch her down the beach; but she was too heavy for them to move her, and her keel sank deep into the sand. Then all the heroes looked at each other blushing; but Jason spoke and said: 'Let us ask the magic bough; perhaps it can help us in our need.'

Then a voice came from the bough, and Jason heard the words it said and bade Orpheus play upon the harp, while the heroes waited round, holding the pine-trunk rollers to help her toward the sea.

Then Orpheus took his harp, and began his magic song: 'How sweet it is to ride upon the surges and to leap from wave to wave, while the wind sings cheerful in the cordage, and the oars flash fast among the foam! How sweet it is to roam across the ocean, and see new towns and wondrous lands, and to come home laden with treasure, and to win undying fame!'

And the good ship *Argo* heard him, and longed to be away and out at sea; till she stirred in every timber and heaved from stem to stern, and leapt up from the sand upon the rollers and plunged onward like a gallant horse; and the heroes fed her path with pine-trunks till she rushed into the whispering sea.

Then they stored her well with food and water and pulled the ladder up on board and settled themselves each men to his oar and kept time to Orpheus' harp; and away across the bay they rowed southward, while the people lined the cliffs; and the women wept, while the men shouted, at the starting of that gallant crew.

PART IV

How the Argonauts Sailed to Colchis

AND what happened next, my children, whether it be true or not, stands written in ancient songs, which you shall read for yourselves some day. And grand old songs they are, written in grand old rolling verse; and they call them the Songs of Orpheus, or the Orphics, to this day. And they tell how the heroes came to Aphetai across the bay and waited for the south-west wind and chose themselves a captain from their crew: and how all called for Heracles, because he was the strongest and most huge, but Heracles refused, and called for Jason, because he was the wisest of them all. So Jason was chosen captain; and Orpheus heaped a pile of

wood, and slew a bull, and offered it to Hera and called all the
heroes to stand round, each man's head crowned with olive,
and to strike their swords into the bull. Then he filled a golden
goblet with the bull's blood and with wheaten flour and honey
and wine and the bitter salt-sea water, and bade the heroes
taste. So each tasted the goblet and passed it round, and vowed
an awful vow: and they vowed before the sun and the night
and the blue-haired sea who shakes the land, to stand by Jason
faithfully in the adventure of the golden fleece; and whosoever
shrank back or disobeyed or turned traitor to his vow, then
justice should minister against him and the Erinnues, who
track guilty men.

Then Jason lighted the pile and burnt the carcass of the bull,
and they went to their ship and sailed eastward like men who
have a work to do; and the place from which they went was
called Aphetai, the sailing-place, from that day forth. Three
thousand years ago and more they sailed away, into the
unknown Eastern seas; and great nations have come and gone
since then, and many a storm has swept the earth, and many a
mighty armament, to which *Argo* would be but one small boat;
English and French, Turkish and Russian, have sailed those
waters since; yet the fame of that small *Argo* lives for ever, and
her name is become a proverb among men.

So they sailed past the Isle of Sciathos, with the Cape of
Sepius on their left, and turned to the northward toward Pelion,
up the long Magnesian shore. On their right hand was the open
sea and on their left old Pelion rose, while the clouds crawled
round his dark pine forests, and his caps of summer snow.
And their hearts yearned for the dear old mountain, as they
thought of pleasant days gone by, and of the sports of their

boyhood, and their hunting, and their schooling in the cave beneath the cliff. And at last Peleus spoke: 'Let us land here, friends, and climb the dear old hill once more. We are going on a fearful journey; who knows if we shall see Pelion again? Let us go up to Cheiron our master, and ask his blessing ere we start. And I have a boy too with him, whom he trains as he trained me once—the son whom Thetis brought me, the silver-footed lady of the sea, whom I caught in the cave, and tamed her, though she changed her shape seven times. For she changed, as I held her, into water, and to vapour, and to burning flame, and to a rock, and to a black-maned lion, and to a tall and stately tree. But I held her and held her ever, till she took her own shape again, and led her to my father's house, and won her for my bride. And all the rulers of Olympus came to our wedding, and the heavens and the earth rejoiced to-gether, when an Immortal wedded mortal man. And now let me see my son, for it is not often I shall see him upon earth; famous he will be, but shortlived, and die in the flower of youth.'

So Tiphys the helmsman steered them to the shore under the crags of Pelion, and they went up through the dark pine forests toward the Centaur's cave.

And they came into the misty hall, beneath the snow-crowned crag, and saw the great Centaur lying, with his huge limbs spread upon the rock; and beside him stood Achilles, the child whom no steel could wound, and played upon his harp right sweetly, while Cheiron watched and smiled.

Then Cheiron leapt up and welcomed them and kissed them every one, and set a feast before them of swine's flesh and venison and good wine; and young Achilles served them, and carried the golden goblet round. And after supper all the heroes clapped their hands, and called on Orpheus to sing; but he refused and said: 'How can I, who am the younger, sing before our ancient host?' So they called on Cheiron to sing, and Achilles brought him his harp, and he began a wondrous song: a famous story of old time, of the fight between the Centaurs and the Lapithai, which you may still see carved in stone.[1] He sang how his brothers came to ruin by their folly, when they were mad with wine; and how they and the heroes fought, with fists and teeth and the goblets from which they drank, and now they tore up the pine trees in their fury and hurled great crags of stone, while the mountains thundered with the battle, and the land was wasted far and wide; till the Lapithai drove them from their home in the rich Thessalian plains to the lonely glens of Pindus, leaving Cheiron all alone. And the heroes praised his song right heartily, for some of them had helped in that great fight.

Then Orpheus took the lyre, and sang of Chaos and the making of the wondrous world, and how all things sprang from Love, who could not live alone in the Abyss. And as he sang his voice rose from the cave, above the crags, and through the tree-tops, and the glens of oak and pine. And the trees bowed their heads when they heard it and the grey rocks cracked and rang, and the forest beasts crept near to listen, and the birds forsook their nests and hovered round. And old Cheiron clapped his hands together and beat his hoofs upon the ground for wonder at that magic song.

Then Peleus kissed his boy and wept over him, and they went down to the ship; and Cheiron came down with them,

[1] In the Elgin Marbles.

weeping, and kissed them one by one and blest them, and promised to them great renown. And the heroes wept when they left him, till their great hearts could weep no more; for he was kind and just and pious, and wiser than all beasts and men. Then he went up to a cliff, and prayed for them that they might come home safe and well, while the heroes rowed away and watched him standing on his cliff above the sea, with his great hands raised toward heaven, and his white locks waving in the wind. And they strained their eyes to watch him to the last, for they felt that they should look on him no more.

So they rowed on over the long swell of the sea, past Olympus, the seat of the Immortals, and past the wooded bays of Athos, and Samothrace the sacred isle; and they came past Lemnos to the Hellespont, and through the narrow strait of Abydos, and so on into the Propontis, which we call Marmora now. And there they met with Cyzicus, ruling in Asia over the Dolions, who the songs say was the son of Aeneas, of whom you will hear many a tale some day. For Homer tells us how he fought at Troy, and Virgil how he sailed away and founded Rome; and men believed until late years that from him sprang our old British kings. Now Cyzicus, the songs say, welcomed the heroes, for his father had been one of Cheiron's scholars; so he welcomed them, and feasted them, and stored their ship with corn and wine, and cloaks and rugs, the songs say, and shirts, of which no doubt they stood in need.

But at night while they lay sleeping, came down on them terrible men, who lived with the bears in the mountains, like Titans or giants in shape, for each of them had six arms, and they fought with young firs and pines. But Heracles killed them all before morn with his deadly poisoned arrows; but

among them, in the darkness, he slew Cyzicus the kindly prince.

Then they got to their ship and to their oars, and Tiphys bade them cast off the hawsers and go to sea. But as he spoke a whirlwind came, and spun the *Argo* round, and twisted the hawsers together, so that no man could loose them. Then Tiphys dropped the rudder from his hand, and cried: 'This comes from the gods above.' But Jason went forward, and asked counsel of the magic bough.

Then the magic bough spoke, and answered: 'This is because you have slain Cyzicus your friend. You must appease his soul or you will never leave this shore.'

Jason went back sadly and told the heroes what he had heard. And they leapt on shore and searched till dawn; and at dawn they found the body, all rolled in dust and blood, among the corpses of those monstrous beasts. And they wept over their kind host and laid him on a fair bed and heaped a huge mound over him and offered black sheep at his tomb, and Orpheus sang a magic song to him, that his spirit might have rest. And then they held games at the tomb, after the custom of those times, and Jason gave prizes to each winner. To Ancaeus he gave a golden cup, for he wrestled best of all; and to Heracles a silver one, for he was the strongest of all; and to Castor, who rode best, a golden crest; and Polydeuces the boxer had a rich carpet; and to Orpheus for his song a sandal with golden wings. But Jason himself was the best of all the archers, and the Minyae crowned him with an olive crown; and so, the songs say, the soul of good Cyzicus was appeased, and the heroes went on their way in peace.

But when Cyzicus' wife heard that he was dead she died likewise of grief, and her tears became a fountain of clear water, which flows the whole year round.

Then they rowed away, the songs say, along the Mysian shore and past the mouth of Rhindacus, till they found a pleasant bay, sheltered by the long ridges of Arganthus and by high walls of basalt rock. And there they ran the ship ashore upon the yellow sand, and furled the sail and took the mast down and lashed it in its crutch. And next they let down the ladder and went ashore to sport and rest.

And there Heracles went away into the woods, bow in hand, to hunt wild deer; and Hylas the fair boy slipt away after him, and followed him by stealth, until he lost himself among the glens, and sat down weary to rest himself by the side of a lake; and there the water nymphs came up to look at him, and loved him, and carried him down under the lake to be their play-fellow, for ever happy and young. And Heracles sought for him in vain, shouting his name till all the mountains rang; but Hylas never heard him far down under the sparkling lake. So while Heracles wandered searching for him, a fair breeze sprang up, and Heracles was nowhere to be found; and the *Argo* sailed away, and Heracles was left behind and never saw the noble Phasian stream.

Then the Minyae came to a doleful land, where Amycus the giant ruled, and cared nothing for the laws of Zeus, but challenged all strangers to box with him, and those whom he conquered he slew. But Polydeuces the boxer struck him a harder blow than he ever felt before and slew him; and the Minyae went on up the Bosphorus, till they came to the city of Phineus, the fierce Bithynian king; for Zetes and Calais bade Jason land there, because they had a work to do.

And they went up from the shore toward the city, through forests white with snow, and Phineus came out to meet them with a lean and woeful face, and said : ' Welcome, gallant heroes, to the land of bitter blasts, the land of cold and misery; yet I will feast you as best I can.' And he led them in and set meat before them, but before they could put their hands to their mouths, down came two fearful monsters, the like of whom man never saw; for they had the faces and the hair of fair maidens, but the wings and claws of hawks; and they snatched the meat from off the table, and flew shrieking out above the roofs.

Then Phineas beat his breast and cried: 'These are the Harpies, whose names are the Whirlwind and the Swift, the daughters of Wonder and of the Amber-nymph, and they rob us night and day. They carried off the daughters of Pandareus, whom all the gods had blest; for Aphrodite fed them on Olympus with honey and milk and wine; and Hera gave them beauty and wisdom, and Athené skill in all the arts; but when they came to their wedding, the Harpies snatched them both away, and gave them to be slaves to the Erinnues, and live in horror all their days. And now they haunt me and my people, and the Bosphorus, with fearful storms, and sweep away our food from off our tables, so that we starve in spite of all our wealth.'

Then up rose Zetes and Calais, the winged sons of the North Wind, and said: 'Do you not know us, Phineus, and these wings which grow upon our backs?' And Phineus hid his face in terror; but he answered not a word.

'Because you have been a traitor, Phineus, the Harpies haunt you night and day. Where is Cleopatra our sister, your wife, whom you keep in prison? And where are her two children, whom you blinded in your rage, at the bidding of an evil woman, and cast them out upon the rocks? Swear to us that you will right our sister, and cast out that wicked woman, and then we will free you from your plague, and drive the whirl-wind maidens to the south; but if not, we will put out your eyes, as you put out the eyes of your own sons.'

Then Phineus swore an oath to them and drove out the wicked woman, and Jason took those two poor children and cured their eyes with magic herbs.

But Zetes and Calais rose up sadly and said: 'Farewell now, heroes all; farewell, our dear companions, with whom we played on Pelion in old times, for a fate is laid upon us and our day is come at last, in which we must hunt the whirlwinds over land and sea for ever; and if we catch them they die, and if not, we die ourselves.'

At that all the heroes wept; but the two young men sprang up and aloft into the air after the Harpies, and the battle of the winds began.

The heroes trembled in silence as they heard the shrieking of the blasts, while the palace rocked and all the city; and great stones were torn from the crags, and the forest pines were hurled earthward, north and south and east and west, and the Bosphorus boiled white with foam, and the clouds were dashed against the cliffs.

But at last the battle ended and the Harpies fled screaming toward the south, and the sons of the North Wind rushed after them and brought clear sunshine where they passed. For many a league they followed them over all the isles of the Cyclades and away to the south-west across Hellas, till they came to the Ionian Sea, and there they fell upon the Echinades, at the mouth of the Achelous; and those isles were called the Whirl-wind Isles for many a hundred years. But what became of Zetes and Calais I know not, for the heroes never saw them again: some say that Heracles met them, and quarrelled with them, and slew them with his arrows; and some say that they fell down from weariness and the heat of the summer sun, and that the Sun god buried them among the Cyclades in the pleasant Isle of Tenos, and for many hundred years their grave was shown there, and over it a pillar, which turned to every wind. But those dark storms and whirlwinds haunt the Bosphorus until this day.

But the Argonauts went eastward, and out into the open sea, which we now call the Black Sea, but it was called the Euxine then. No Hellene had ever crossed it, and all feared that dreadful sea and its rocks and shoals and fogs and bitter freezing storms;

and they told strange stories of it, some false and some half-true—how it stretched northward to the ends of the earth, and the sluggish Putrid Sea, and the everlasting night, and the regions of the dead. So the heroes trembled, for all their courage, as they came into that wild Black Sea, and saw it stretching out before them, without a shore, as far as eye could see.

And first Orpheus spoke, and warned them: 'We shall come now to the wandering blue rocks; my mother warned me of them, Calliope, the immortal muse.'

And soon they saw the blue rocks shining like spires and castles of grey glass, while an ice-cold wind blew from them and chilled all the heroes' hearts. And as they neared they could see them heaving, as they rolled upon the long sea-waves, crashing and grinding together till the roar went up to heaven. The sea sprang up in spouts between them and swept round them in white sheets of foam; but their heads swung nodding high in air, while the wind whistled shrill among the crags.

The heroes' hearts sank within them and they lay upon their oars in fear, but Orpheus called to Tiphys the helmsman: 'Between them we must pass; so look ahead for an opening, and be brave, for Hera is with us.' But Tiphys the cunning helmsman stood silent, clenching his teeth, till he saw a heron come flying mast-high toward the rocks, and hover awhile before them, as if looking for a passage through. Then he cried: 'Hera has sent us a pilot; let us follow the cunning bird.'

Then the heron flapped to and fro for a moment till he saw a hidden gap, and into it he rushed like an arrow, while the heroes watched what would befall.

And the blue rocks clashed together as the bird fled swiftly

See page 85

THE HEROES WERE AWED BEFORE AIETES AS HE SHONE
IN HIS CHARIOT

through; but they struck but a feather from his tail and then rebounded apart at the shock.

Then Tiphys cheered the heroes and they shouted, and the oars bent like withes beneath their strokes as they rushed between those toppling ice-crags and the cold blue lips of death. And ere the rocks could meet again they had passed them and were safe out in the open sea.

And after that they sailed on wearily along the Asian coast, by the Black Cape and Thyneis, where the hot stream of Thymbris falls into the sea, and Sangarius, whose waters float on the Euxine, till they came to Wolf the river, and to Wolf the kindly king. And there died two brave heroes, Idmon, and Tiphys the wise helmsman: one died of an evil sickness and one a wild boar slew. So the heroes heaped a mound above them and set upon it an oar on high, and left them there to sleep together, on the far-off Lycian shore. But Idas killed the boar and avenged Tiphys, and Ancaios took the rudder and was helmsman and steered them on toward the east.

And they went on past Sinope and many a mighty river's mouth, and past many a barbarous tribe and the cities of the Amazons, the warlike women of the east, till all night they heard the clank of anvils and the roar of furnace blasts, and the forge fires shone like sparks through the darkness in the mountain glens aloft; for they were come to the shores of the Chalybes, the smiths who never tire, but serve Ares the cruel war god, forging weapons day and night.

And at day-dawn they looked eastward, and midway between the sea and the sky they saw white snow-peaks hanging, glittering sharp and bright above the clouds. And they knew that they were come to Caucasus, at the end of all the earth—Caucasus the highest of all mountains, the father of the rivers of the east. On his peak lies chained the Titan, Prometheus, while a vulture tears his heart, and at his feet are piled dark forests round the magic Colchian land.

And they rowed three days to the eastward while Caucasus rose higher hour by hour, till they saw the dark stream of Phasis rushing headlong to the sea and, shining above the tree-tops, the golden roofs of King Aietes, the child of the Sun.

Then out spoke Ancaios the helmsman: 'We are come to our goal at last, for there are the roofs of Aieties, and the woods where all poisons grow; but who can tell us where among them is hid the golden fleece? Many a toil must we bear ere we find it, and bring it home to Greece.'

But Jason cheered the heroes, for his heart was high and bold, and he said: 'I will go alone up to Aietes, though he be the child of the Sun, and win him with soft words. Better so than to go all together, and to come to blows at once.' But the Minyae would not stay behind, so they rowed boldly up the stream.

And a dream came to Aietes, and filled his heart with fear. He thought he saw a shining star, which fell into his daughter's lap; and that Medeia his daughter took it gladly, and carried it to the riverside and cast it in, and there the whirling river bore it down and out into the Euxine Sea.

Then he leapt up in fear, and bade his servants bring his chariot, that he might go down to the riverside and appease the nymphs, and the heroes whose spirits haunt the bank. So he went down in his golden chariot, and his daughters by his side —Medeia the fair witch-maiden, and Chalciope, who had been

Phrixus' wife—and behind him a crowd of servants and soldiers, for he was a rich and a mighty prince.

And as he drove down by the reedy river he saw *Argo* sliding up beneath the bank, and many a hero in her, like Immortals for beauty and for strength, as their weapons glittered round them in the level morning sunlight, through the white mist of the stream. But Jason was the noblest of all; for Hera, who loved him, gave him beauty and tallness and terrible manhood.

And when they came near together and looked into each other's eyes the heroes were awed before Aietes as he shone in his chariot, like his father the glorious Sun; for his robes were of rich gold tissue, and the rays of his diadem flashed fire. And in his hand he bore a jewelled sceptre, which glittered like the stars; and sternly he looked at them under his brows, and sternly he spoke and loud:

'Who are you, and what want you here, that you come to the shore of Cutaia? Do you take no account of my rule, nor of my people the Colchians who serve me, who never tired yet in the battle and know well how to face an invader?'

And the heroes sat silent awhile before the face of that ancient king. But Hera the awful goddess put courage into Jason's heart, and he rose and shouted loudly in answer: 'We are no pirates nor lawless men. We come not to plunder and to ravage, or carry away slaves from your land. But my uncle, the son of Poseidon, Pelias the Minyan king—he it is who has set me on a quest to bring home the golden fleece. And these too, my bold comrades, they are no nameless men; for some are the sons of Immortals, and some of heroes far renowned. And we too never tire in battle and know well how to give blows and to take. Yet we wish to be guests at your table: it will be better so for both.'

Then Aietes' rage rushed up like a whirlwind, and his eyes flashed fire as he heard; but he crushed his anger down in his breast, and spoke mildly a cunning speech:

'If you will fight for the fleece with my Colchians, then many a man must die. But do you indeed expect to win from me the fleece in fight? So few you are that if you be worsted I can load the ship with your corpses. But if you will be ruled by me, you will find it better far to choose the best man among you and let him fulfil the labours which I demand. Then I will give him the golden fleece for a prize and a glory to you all.'

So saying, he turned his horses and drove back in silence to the town. And the Minyae sat silent with sorrow and longed for Heracles and his strength; for there was no facing the thousands of the Colchians and the fearful chance of war.

But Chalciope, Phrixus' widow, went weeping to the town, for she remembered her Minyan husband, and all the pleasures of her youth, while she watched the fair faces of his kinsmen, and their long locks of golden hair. And she whispered to Medeia her sister: 'Why should all these brave men die? Why does not my father give them up the fleece, that my husband's spirit may have rest?'

And Medeia's heart pitied the heroes, and Jason most of all; and she answered: 'Our father is stern and terrible, and who can win the golden fleece?' But Chalciope said: 'These men are not like our men; there is nothing which they cannot dare nor do.'

And Medeia thought of Jason and his brave countenance, and said: 'If there was one among them who knew no fear, I could show him how to win the fleece.'

So in the dusk of evening they went down to the riverside, Chalciope and Medeia the witch-maiden, and Argus, Phrixus' son. And Argus the boy crept forward, among the beds of reeds, till he came where the heroes were sleeping, on the thwarts of the ship, beneath the bank, while Jason kept ward on shore, and leant upon his lance full of thought. And the boy came to Jason and said:

'I am the son of Phrixus, your cousin, and Chalciope my mother waits for you, to talk about the golden fleece.'

Then Jason went boldly with the boy, and found the two princesses standing; and when Chalciope saw him she wept, and took his hands, and cried:

'O cousin of my beloved, go home before you die!'

'It would be base to go home now, fair princess, and to have sailed all these seas in vain.' Then both the princesses besought him; but Jason said: 'It is too late.'

'But you know not,' said Medeia, 'what he must do who would win the fleece. He must tame the two brazen-footed bulls, who breathe devouring flame, and with them he must plough ere nightfall four acres in the field of Ares, and he must sow them with serpents' teeth, of which each tooth springs up into an armed man. Then he must fight with all those warriors; and little will it profit him to conquer them, for the fleece is guarded by a serpent, more huge than any mountain pine; and over his body you must step if you would reach the golden fleece.'

Then Jason laughed bitterly. 'Unjustly is that fleece kept here, and by an unjust and lawless king; and unjustly shall I die in my youth, for I will attempt it ere another sun be set.'

Then Medeia trembled, and said: 'No mortal man can reach

that fleece unless I guide him through. For round it, beyond
the river, is a wall full nine ells high with lofty towers and but-
tresses, and mighty gates of threefold brass; and over the gates
the wall is arched, with golden battlements above. And over
the gateway sits Brimo, the wild witch-huntress of the woods,
brandishing a pine-torch in her hands, while her mad hounds
howl around. No man dare meet her or look on her, but only I
her priestess, and she watches far and wide lest any stranger
should come near.'

'No wall so high but it may be climbed at last, and no wood
so thick but it may be crawled through; no serpent so wary but
he may be charmed, or witch-queen so fierce but spells may
soothe her; and I may yet win the golden fleece, if a wise
maiden help bold men.'

And he looked at Medeia cunningly, and held her with his
glittering eye, till she blushed and trembled, and said:

'Who can face the fire of the bull's breath, and fight ten
thousand armed men?'

'He whom you help,' said Jason, flattering her, 'for your
fame is spread over all the earth. Are you not the queen of all
enchantresses, wiser even than your sister Circe, in her fairy
island in the west?'

'Would that I were with my sister Circe in her fairy island
in the west, far away from sore temptation and thoughts which
tear the heart! But if it must be so—for why should you die?—
I have an ointment here; I made it from the magic ice-flower
which sprang from Prometheus' wound, above the clouds on
Caucasus, in the dreary fields of snow. Anoint yourself with
that, and you shall have in you seven men's strength; and
anoint your shield with it, and neither fire nor sword can harm

you. But what you begin you must end before sunset, for its virtue lasts only one day. And anoint your helmet with it before you sow the serpents' teeth; and when the sons of earth spring up, cast your helmet among their ranks, and the deadly crop of the war god's field will mow itself, and perish.'

Then Jason fell on his knees before her, and thanked her and kissed her hands; and she gave him the vase of ointment, and fled trembling through the reeds. And Jason told his comrades what had happened and showed them the box of ointment, and all rejoiced but Idas, and he grew mad with envy.

And at sunrise Jason went and bathed, and anointed himself from head to foot and his shield and his helmet and his weapons, and bade his comrades try the spell. So they tried to bend his lance, but it stood like an iron bar; and Idas in spite hewed at it with his sword, but the blade flew to splinters in his face. Then they hurled their lances at his shield, but the spear-points turned like lead; and Caineus tried to throw him, but he never stirred a foot; and Polydeuces struck him with his fist a blow which would have killed an ox, but Jason only smiled, and the heroes danced about him with delight; and he leapt and ran and shouted in the joy of that enormous strength, till the sun rose and it was time to go and to claim Aietes' promise.

So he sent up Telamon and Aithalides to tell Aietes that he was ready for the fight; and they went up among the marble walls and beneath the roofs of gold, and stood in Aietes' hall, while he grew pale with rage.

'Fulfil your promise to us, child of the blazing Sun. Give us the serpents' teeth and let loose the fiery bulls, for we have found a champion among us who can win the golden fleece.'

And Aietes bit his lips, for he fancied that they had fled away by night; but he could not go back from his promise, so he gave them the serpents' teeth.

Then he called for his chariot and his horses and sent heralds through all the town; and all the people went out with him to the dreadful war god's field.

And there Aietes sat upon his throne, with his warriors on each hand, thousands and tens of thousands, clothed from head to foot in steel chain-mail. And the people and the women

crowded to every window and bank and wall; while the Minyae stood together, a mere handful in the midst of that great host.

And Chalciope was there and Argus, trembling, and Medeia, wrapped closely in her veil; but Aietes did not know that she was muttering cunning spells between her lips.

Then Jason cried: 'Fulfil your promise, and let your fiery bulls come forth.'

Then Aietes bade open the gates, and the magic bulls leapt out. Their brazen hoofs rang upon the ground and their nostrils sent out sheets of flame, as they rushed with lowered heads upon Jason; but he never flinched a step. The flame of their breath swept round him, but it singed not a hair of his head;

and the bulls stopped short and trembled when Medeia began
her spell.

Then Jason sprang upon the nearest and seized him by the
horns; and up and down they wrestled, till the bull fell grovel-
ling on his knees; for the heart of the brute died with him and
his mighty limbs were loosed, beneath the steadfast eye of that
dark witch-maiden and
the magic whisper of
her lips.

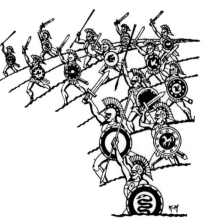

So both the bulls
were tamed and yoked;
and Jason bound them
to the plough and
goaded them onward
with his lance till he
had ploughed the sacred
field.

And all the Minyae
shouted; but Aietes bit

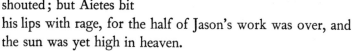

his lips with rage, for the half of Jason's work was over, and
the sun was yet high in heaven.

Then he took the serpents' teeth and sowed them and waited
what would befall. But Medeia looked at him and at his helmet,
lest he should forget the lesson she had taught.

And every furrow heaved and bubbled, and out of every clod
arose a man. Out of the earth they rose by thousands, each
clad from head to foot in steel, and drew their swords and
rushed on Jason, where he stood in the midst alone.

Then the Minyae grew pale with fear for him, but Aietes
laughed a bitter laugh. 'See! if I had not warriors enough

already round me, I could call them out of the bosom of the earth.'

But Jason snatched off his helmet and hurled it into the thickest of the throng. And blind madness came upon them, suspicion, hate and fear; and one cried to his fellow: 'Thou didst strike me!' and another: 'Thou art Jason—thou shalt die!' So fury seized those earth-born phantoms, and each turned his hand against the rest; and they fought and were never weary, till they all lay dead upon the ground. Then the magic furrows opened, and the kind earth took them home into her breast, and the grass grew up all green again above them, and Jason's work was done.

Then the Minyae rose and shouted, till Prometheus heard them from his crag. And Jason cried: 'Lead me to the fleece this moment, before the sun goes down.'

But Aietes thought: 'He has conquered the bulls, and sown and reaped the deadly crop. Who is this who is proof against all magic? He may kill the serpent yet.' So he delayed and sat taking counsel with his princes till the sun went down and all was dark. Then he bade a herald cry: 'Every man to his home for tonight. Tomorrow we will meet these heroes and speak about the golden fleece.'

Then he turned and looked at Medeia: 'This is your doing, false witch-maid! You have helped these yellow-haired strangers, and brought shame upon your father and yourself!'

Medeia shrank and trembled, and her face grew pale with fear, and Aietes knew that she was guilty, and whispered: 'If they win the fleece, you die!'

But the Minyae marched toward their ship, growling like lions cheated of their prey, for they saw that Aietes meant to mock them and to cheat them out of all their toil. And Oileus said: 'Let us go to the grove together and take the fleece by force.'

And Idas the rash cried: 'Let us draw lots who shall go in first; for while the dragon is devouring one, the rest can slay him and carry off the fleece in peace.' But Jason held them back, though he praised them, for he hoped for Medeia's help.

And after a while Medeia came trembling, and wept a long while before she spoke. And at last:

'My end is come and I must die; for my father has found out that I have helped you. You he would kill if he dared, but he will not harm you, because you have been his guests. Go then, go, and remember poor Medeia when you are far away across the sea.' But all the heroes cried:

'If you die, we die with you; for without you we cannot win the fleece, and home we will not go without it, but fall here fighting to the last man.'

'You need not die,' said Jason. 'Flee home with us across the sea. Show us first how to win the fleece, for you can do it. Why else are you the priestess of the grove? Show us but how to win the fleece and come with us, and you shall be my queen and rule over the rich princes of the Minyae, in Iolcos by the sea.'

And all the heroes pressed round and vowed to her that she should be their queen.

Medeia wept and shuddered and hid her face in her hands; for her heart yearned after her sisters and her playfellows, and the home where she was brought up as a child. But at last she looked up at Jason, and spoke between her sobs:

'Must I leave my home and my people, to wander with

strangers across the sea? The lot is cast and I must endure it. I will show you how to win the golden fleece. Bring up your ship to the wood-side and moor her there against the bank, and let Jason come up at midnight and one brave comrade with him, and meet me beneath the wall.'

Then all the heroes cried together: 'I will go!', 'And I!', 'And I!' And Idas the rash grew mad with envy, for he longed to be foremost in all things. But Medeia calmed them, and said: 'Orpheus shall go with Jason, and bring his magic harp; for I hear of him that he is the king of all minstrels, and can charm all things on earth.'

And Orpheus laughed for joy and clapped his hands, because the choice had fallen on him; for in those days poets and singers were as bold warriors as the best.

So at midnight they went up the bank, and found Medeia; and beside came Absyrtus her young brother, leading a yearling lamb.

Then Medeia brought them to a thicket beside the war god's gate; and there she bade Jason dig a ditch, and kill the lamb and leave it there, and strew on it magic herbs and honey from the honeycomb.

Then sprang up through the earth with the red fire flashing before her, Brimo the wild witch-huntress, while her mad hounds howled around. She had one head like a horse's and another like a ravening hound's and another like a hissing snake's, and a sword in either hand. And she leapt into the ditch with her hounds, and they ate and drank their fill, while Jason and Orpheus trembled, and Medeia hid her eyes. And at last the witch-queen vanished and fled with her hounds into the woods, and the bars of the gates fell down, and the brazen doors flew wide, and Medeia and the heroes ran forward and hurried through the poison wood, among the dark stems of the mighty beeches, guided by the gleam of the golden fleece, until they saw it hanging on one vast tree in the midst. And Jason would have sprung to seize it; but Medeia held him back and pointed, shuddering, to the tree-foot, where the mighty serpent lay, coiled in and out among the roots, with a body like a mountain pine. His coils stretched many a fathom, spangled with bronze and gold; and half of him they could see, but no more, for the rest lay in the darkness far beyond.

And when he saw them coming he lifted up his head and watched them with his small bright eyes, and flashed his forked tongue, and roared like the fire among the woodlands, till the forest tossed and groaned. For his cries shook the trees from leaf to root, and swept over the long reaches of the river and over Aietes' hall, and woke the sleepers in the city, till mothers clasped their children in their fear.

But Medeia called gently to him, and he stretched out his long spotted neck and licked her hand and looked up in her face, as if to ask for food. Then she made a sign to Orpheus, and he began his magic song.

And as he sang, the forest grew calm again, and the leaves on every tree hung still; and the serpent's head sank down and his brazen coils grew limp and his glittering eyes closed lazily, till he breathed as gently as a child, while Orpheus called to pleasant Slumber, who gives peace to men and beasts and waves.

Then Jason leapt forward warily, and stept across that mighty snake, and tore the fleece from off the tree-trunk; and the four rushed down the garden, to the bank where the *Argo* lay.

There was a silence for a moment, while Jason held the golden fleece on high. Then he cried: 'Go now, good *Argo*, swift and steady, if ever you would see Pelion more.'

And she went as the heroes drove her grim and silent all, with muffled oars, till the pine-wood bent like willow in their hands, and stout *Argo* groaned beneath their strokes.

On and on, beneath the dewy darkness, they fled swiftly down the swirling stream; underneath black walls and temples and the castles of the princes of the east, past sluice-mouths and fragrant gardens and groves of all strange fruits, past marshes where fat kine lay sleeping, and long beds of whispering reeds; till they heard the merry music of the surge upon the bar, as it tumbled in the moonlight all alone.

Into the surge they rushed, and *Argo* leapt the breakers like a horse; for she knew the time was come to show her mettle and win honour for the heroes and herself.

Into the surge they rushed, and *Argo* leapt the breakers like a horse, till the heroes stopped all panting, each man upon his oar, as she slid into the still broad sea.

Then Orpheus took his harp and sang a paean, till the heroes' hearts rose high again; and they rowed on stoutly and steadfastly, away into the darkness of the west.

PART V

How the Argonauts were Driven into the Unknown Sea

So they fled away in haste to the westward; but Aietes manned his fleet and followed them. And Lynceus the quick-eyed saw him coming, while he was still many a mile away, and cried: 'I see a hundred ships, like a flock of white swans, far in the east.' And at that they rowed hard, like heroes; but the ships came nearer every hour.

Then Medeia, the dark witch-maiden, laid a cruel and a cunning plot; for she killed Absyrtus her young brother, and cast him into the sea, and said: 'Ere my father can take up his corpse and bury it, he must wait long, and be left far behind.'

And all the heroes shuddered, and looked one at the other for shame; yet they did not punish that dark witch-woman, because she had won for them the golden fleece.

And when Aietes came to the place he saw the floating

corpse; and he stopped a long while and bewailed his son and took him up, and went home. But he sent on his sailors towards the westward, and bound them by a mighty curse: 'Bring back to me that dark witch-woman, that she may die a dreadful death. But if you return without her, you shall die by the same death yourselves.'

So the Argonauts escaped for that time: but Father Zeus saw that foul crime; and out of the heavens he sent a storm, and swept the ship far from her course. Day after day the storm drove her amid foam and blinding mist, till they knew no longer where they were, for the sun was blotted from the skies. And at last the ship struck on a shoal, amid low isles of mud and sand, and the waves rolled over her and through her, and the heroes lost all hope of life.

Then Jason cried to Hera: 'Fair queen, who hast befriended us till now, why hast thou left us in our misery, to die here among unknown seas? It is hard to lose the honour which we have wone with such toil and danger, and hard never to see Hellas again, and the pleasant bay of Pagasai.'

Then out and spoke the magic bough which stood upon the *Argo*'s beak: 'Because Father Zeus is angry, all this has fallen on you; for a cruel crime has been done on board and the sacred ship is foul with blood.'

At that some of the heroes cried: 'Medeia is the murderess. Let the witch-woman bear her sin and die!' And they seized Medeia, to hurl her into the sea, and atone for the young boy's death; but the magic bough spoke again: 'Let her live till her crimes are full. Vengeance waits for her, slow and sure; but she must live, for you need her still. She must show you the way to her sister Circe, who lives among the islands of the west. To her you must sail, a weary way, and she shall cleanse you from your guilt.'

Then all the heroes wept aloud when they heard the sentence of the oak; for they knew that a dark journey lay before them, and years of bitter toil. And some upbraided the dark witch-woman, and some said, : 'Nay, we are her debtors still; without her we should never have won the fleece.' But most of them bit their lips in silence, for they feared the witch's spells.

And now the sea grew calmer and the sun shone out once more, and the heroes thrust the ship off the sand-bank, and rowed forward on their weary course under the guiding of the dark witch-maiden, into the wastes of the unknown sea.

Whither they went I cannot tell, nor how they came to Circe's isle. Some say that they went to the westward, and up the Ister [1] stream, and so came into the Adriatic, dragging their ship over the snowy Alps. And others say that they went southward, into the Red Indian Sea, and past the sunny lands where spices grow, round Aethiopia toward the west; and that at last they came to Libya and dragged their ship across the burning sands, and over the hills into the Syrtes, where the flats and quicksands spread for many a mile, between rich Cyrene and the Lotus-eaters' shore. But all these are but dreams and fables, and dim hints of unknown lands.

But all say that they came to a place where they had to drag their ship across the land nine days with ropes and rollers, till they came into an unknown sea. And the best of all the old songs tells us how they went away toward the north, till they came to the slope of Caucasus, where it sinks into the sea; and to the narrow Cimmerian Bosphorus,[2] where the Titan swam

---

[1] The Danube.   [2] Between the Crimea and Circassia.

across upon the bull; and thence into the lazy waters of the still Maeotid lake.[1] And thence they went northward ever, up the Tanais, which we call Don, past the Geloni and Sauromatai, and many a wandering shepherd-tribe, and the one-eyed Arimaspi, of whom old Greek poets tell, who steal the gold from the Griffins, in the cold Riphaian hills.[2]

And they passed the Scythian archers and the Tauri who eat men, and the wandering Hyperboreai, who feed their flocks beneath the pole-star, until they came into the northern ocean, the dull dead Cronian Sea.[3] And there *Argo* would move on no longer; and each man clasped his elbow and leaned his head upon his hand, heartbroken with toil and hunger, and gave himself up to death. But brave Ancaios the helmsman cheered up their hearts once more, and bade them leap on land and haul the ship with ropes and rollers for many a weary day, whether over land or mud or ice, I know not, for the song is mixed and broken like a dream. And it says next, how they came to the rich nation of the famous long-lived men, and to the coast of the Cimmerians, who never saw the sun, buried deep in the glens of the snow mountains, and to the fair land of Hermione, where dwelt the most righteous of all nations, and to the gates of the world below, and to the dwelling-place of dreams.

And at last Ancaios shouted: 'Endure a little while, brave friends, the worst is surely past; for I can see the pure west wind ruffle the water and hear the roar of ocean on the sands. So raise up the mast and set the sail and face what comes like men.'

Then out spoke the magic bough: 'Ah, would that I had

---

[1] The Sea of Azov.   [2] The Ural Mountains?
          [3] The Baltic?

perished long ago, and been whelmed by the dread blue rocks, beneath the fierce swell of the Euxine! Better so, than to wander for ever, disgraced by the guilt of my princes; for the blood of Absyrtus still tracks me, and woe follows hard upon woe. And now some dark horror will clutch me, if I come near the isle of Ierne.[1] Unless you will cling to the land and sail southward and southward for ever, I shall wander beyond the Atlantic, to the ocean which has no shore.'

Then they blest the magic bough and sailed southward along the land. But ere they could pass Ierne, the land of mists and storms, the wild wind came down, dark and roaring, and caught the sail, and strained the ropes. And away they drove twelve nights, on the wide wild western sea, through the foam and over the rollers, while they saw neither sun nor stars. And they cried again: 'We shall perish, for we know not where we are. We are lost in the dreary damp darkness and cannot tell north from south.'

But Lynceus the long-sighted called gaily from the bows: 'Take heart again, brave sailors, for I see a pine-clad isle, and the halls of the kind Earth-mother, with a crown of clouds around them.'

But Orpheus said: 'Turn from them, for no living man can land there: there is no harbour on the coast, but steep-walled cliffs all round.'

So Ancaios turned the ship away, and for three days more they sailed on, till they came to Aiaia, Circe's home, and the fairy island of the west.[2]

And there Jason bid them land, and seek about for any sign of living man. And as they went inland Circe met them, coming

---

[1] Britain?   [2] The Azores?

down toward the ship; and they trembled when they saw her, for her hair and face and robes shone like flame.

And she came and looked at Medeia; and Medeia hid her face beneath her veil.

And Circe cried: 'Ah, wretched girl, have you forgotten all your sins, that you come hither to my island, where the flowers bloom all the year round? Where is your aged father, and the brother whom you killed? Little do I expect you to return in safety with these strangers whom you love. I will send you food and wine, but your ship must not stay here, for it is foul with sin, and foul with sin its crew.'

And the heroes prayed her, but in vain, and cried: 'Cleanse us from our guilt!' But she sent them away, and said: 'Go on to Malea, and there you may be cleansed and return home.'

Then a fair wind rose, and they sailed eastward, by Tartessus on the Iberian shore, till they came to the Pillars of Heracles and the Mediterranean Sea. And thence they sailed on through the deeps of Sardinia and past the Ausonian islands and the capes of the Tyrrhenian shore, till they came to a flowery island, upon a still bright summer's eve. And as they neared it, slowly and wearily, they heard sweet songs upon the shore. But when Medeia heard it, she started, and cried: 'Beware, all heroes, for these are the rocks of the Sirens. You must pass close by them, for there is no other channel; but those who listen to that song are lost.'

Then Orpheus spoke, the king of all minstrels: 'Let them match their song against mine. I have charmed stones and trees and dragons; how much more the hearts of men!' So he caught up his lyre and stood upon the poop, and began his magic song.

And now they could see the Sirens on Anthemousa, the

flowery isle; three fair maidens sitting on the beach, beneath a red rock in the setting sun, among beds of crimson poppies and golden asphodel. Slowly they sang and sleepily, with silver voices, mild and clear, which stole over the golden waters, and into the hearts of all the heroes, in spite of Orpheus' song.

And all things stayed around and listened; the gulls sat in white lines along the rocks; on the beach great seals lay basking, and kept time with lazy heads; while silver shoals of fish came up to hearken, and whispered as they broke the shining calm. The Wind overhead hushed his whistling, as he shepherded his clouds toward the west; and the clouds stood in mid blue, and listened dreaming, like a flock of golden sheep.

And as the heroes listened, the oars fell from their hands, and their heads drooped on their breasts, and they closed their heavy eyes; and they dreamed of bright still gardens, and of slumbers under murmuring pines, till all their toil seemed foolishness, and they thought of their renown no more.

Then one lifted his head suddenly, and cried: 'What use in wandering for ever? Let us stay here and rest awhile.' And another: 'Let us row to the shore, and hear the words they sing.' And another: 'I care not for the words, but for the music. They shall sing me to sleep, that I may rest.'

And Butes, the son of Pandion, the fairest of all mortal men, leapt out and swam toward the shore, crying: 'I come, I come, fair maidens, to live and die here, listening to your song.'

Then Medeia clapped her hands together, and cried: 'Sing louder, Orpheus, sing a bolder strain; wake up these hapless sluggards, or none of them will see the land of Hellas more.'

Then Orpheus lifted his harp, and crashed his cunning hand

across the strings; and his music and his voice rose like a trumpet through the still evening air. Into the air it rushed like thunder, till the rocks rang and the sea, and into their souls it rushed like wine till all hearts beat fast within their breasts.

And he sang the song of Perseus, how the gods led him over land and sea, and how he slew the loathly Gorgon and won himself a peerless bride, and how he sits now with the gods upon Olympus, a shining star in the sky, immortal with his immortal bride, and honoured by all men below.

So Orpheus sang, and the Sirens, answering each other across the golden sea, till Orpheus' voice drowned the Sirens', and the heroes caught their oars again.

And they cried: 'We will be men like Perseus, and we will dare and suffer to the last. Sing us his song again, brave Orpheus, that we may forget the Sirens and their spell.'

And as Orpheus sang, they dashed their oars into the sea, and kept time to his music, as they fled fast away; and the Sirens' voices died behind them, in the hissing of the foam along their wake.

But Butes swam to the shore, and knelt down before the Sirens, and cried: 'Sing on! sing on!' But he could say no more, for a charmed sleep came over him and a pleasant humming in his ears, and he sank all along upon the pebbles, and forgot all heaven and earth, and never looked at that sad beach around him, all strewn with the bones of men.

Then slowly rose up those three fair sisters with a cruel smile upon their lips, and slowly they crept down towards him, like leopards who creep upon their prey; and their hands were like the talons of eagles as they stept across the bones of their victims to enjoy their cruel feast.

But fairest Aphrodite saw him from the highest Idalian peak, and she pitied his youth and his beauty and leapt up from her golden throne, and like a falling star she cleft the sky and left a trail of glittering light, till she stooped to the Isle of the Sirens and snatched their prey from their claws. And she lifted Butes as he lay sleeping and wrapt him in a golden mist, and she bore him to the peak of Lilybaeum, and he slept there many a pleasant year.

But when the Sirens saw that they were conquered, they shrieked for envy and rage, and leapt from the beach into the sea, and were changed into rocks until this day.

Then they came to the straits by Lilybaeum and saw Sicily, the three-cornered island—under which Enceladus the giant lies groaning day and night, and when he turns the earth quakes and his breath bursts out in roaring flames from the highest cone of Aetna, above the chestnut woods. And there Charybdis caught them in its fearful coils of wave, and rolled mast-high about them and spun them round and round, and they could go neither back nor forward while the whirlpool sucked them in.

And while they struggled they saw near them, on the other

side the strait, a rock stand in the water, with its peak wrapt round in clouds—a rock which no man could climb, though he had twenty hands and feet, for the stone was smooth and slippery, as if polished by man's hand; and half way up a misty cave looked out toward the west.

And when Orpheus saw it he groaned, and struck his hands together. And, 'Little will it help us', he cried, 'to escape the jaws of the whirlpool, for in that cave lives Scylla, the sea hag with a young whelp's voice. My mother warned me of her ere we sailed away from Hellas; she has six heads and six long necks, and hides in that dark cleft. And from her cave she fishes for all things which pass by—for sharks and seals and dolphins, and all the herds of Amphitrite. And never ship's crew boasted that they came safe by her rock, and she bends her long necks down to them, and every mouth takes up a man. And who will help us now? For Hera and Zeus hate us, and our ship is foul with guilt; so we must die, whatever befalls.'

Then out of the depths came Thetis, Peleus' silver-footed bride, for love of her gallant husband, and all her nymphs around her; and they played like snow-white dolphins, diving on from wave to wave, before the ship and in her wake and beside her, as dolphins play. And they caught the ship and guided her and passed her on from hand to hand, and tossed her through the billows, as maidens toss the ball. And when Scylla stooped to seize her, they struck back her ravening heads, and foul Scylla whined, as a whelp whines, at the touch of their gentle hands. But she shrank into her cave affrighted—for all bad things shrink from good—and *Argo* leapt safe past her, while a fair breeze rose behind. Then Thetis and her nymphs sank down to their coral caves beneath the sea, and their gardens of green and purple, where live flowers bloom all the year round; while the heroes went on rejoicing, yet dreading what might come next.

After that they rowed on steadily for many a weary day, till they saw a long high island, and beyond it a mountain land. And they searched till they found a harbour, and there rowed boldly in. But after a while they stopped and wondered, for there stood a great city on the shore, and temples and walls and gardens, and castles high in air upon the cliffs. And on either side they saw a harbour with a narrow mouth, but wide within, and black ships without number, high and dry upon the shore.

Then Ancaios, the wise helmsman, spoke: 'What new wonder is this? I know all isles and harbours, and the windings of all seas; and this should be Corcyra, where a few wild goat-herds dwell. But whence come these new harbours and vast works of polished stone?'

But Jason said: 'They can be no savage people. We will go in and take our chance.'

So they rowed into the harbour among a thousand black-beaked ships, each larger far than *Argo*, toward a quay of polished stone. And they wondered at that mighty city, with its roofs of burnished brass and long and lofty walls of marble, with strong palisades above. And the quays were full of people —merchants and mariners and slaves—going to and fro with merchandise among the crowd of ships. And the heroes' hearts were humbled, and they looked at each other and said: 'We thought ourselves a gallant crew when we sailed from Iolcos by the sea, but how small we look before this city, like an ant before a hive of bees.'

Then the sailors hailed them roughly from the quay: 'What men are you? We want no strangers here, nor pirates. We keep our business to ourselves.'

But Jason answered gently, with many a flattering word, and praised their city and their harbour and their fleet of gallant ships. 'Surely you are the children of Poseidon and the masters of the sea; and we are but poor wandering mariners, worn out with thirst and toil. Give us but food and water and we will go on our voyage in peace.'

Then the sailors laughed and answered: 'Stranger, you are no fool; you talk like an honest man, and you shall find us honest too. We are the children of Poseidon, and the masters of the sea; but come ashore to us, and you shall have the best that we can give.'

So they limped ashore, all stiff and weary, with long ragged beards and sunburnt cheeks, and garments torn and weather-stained, and weapons rusted with the spray, while the sailors laughed at them, for they were rough-tongued, though their hearts were frank and kind. And one said: 'These fellows are but raw sailors; they look as if they had been seasick all the day.' And another: 'Their legs have grown crooked with much rowing, till they waddle in their walk like ducks.'

At that Idas the rash would have struck them, but Jason held him back, till one of the merchant kings spoke to them, a tall and stately man.

'Do not be angry, strangers; the sailor boys must have their jest. But we will treat you justly and kindly, for strangers and poor men come from God, and you seem no common sailors by your strength and height and weapons. Come up with me to the palace of Alcinous, the rich seagoing king, and we will feast you well and heartily; and after that you shall tell us your name.'

But Medeia hung back and trembled and whispered in Jason's ear: 'We are betrayed and are going to our ruin, for I see my countrymen among the crowd—dark-eyed Colchi in steel mail-shirts, such as they wear in my father's land.'

'It is too late to turn,' said Jason. And he spoke to the merchant king: 'What country is this, good sir? And what is this new-built town?'

'This is the land of the Phaeaces, beloved by all the Immortals; for they come hither and feast like friends with us and sit by our side in the hall. Hither we came from Liburnia to escape the unrighteous Cyclopes, for they robbed us, peaceful merchants, of our hard-earned wares and wealth. So Nausithous, the son of Poseidon, brought us hither, and died in peace; and now his son Alcinous rules us, and Arete the wisest of queens.'

So they went up across the square, and wondered still more as they went; for along the quays lay in order great cables and yards and masts, before the fair temple of Poseidon, the blue-haired king of the seas. And round the square worked the shipwrights—as many in number as ants—twining ropes and hewing timber and smoothing long yards and oars. And the Minyae went on in silence through clean white marble streets till they came to the hall of Alcinous, and they wondered then still more. For the lofty palace shone aloft in the sun, with walls of plated brass from the threshold to the innermost chamber, and the doors were of silver and gold. And on each side of the doorway sat living dogs of gold, who never grew old or died, so well Hephaistos had made them in his forges in smoking

Lemnos, and gave them to Alcinous to guard his gates by night. And within, against the walls, stood thrones on either side, down the whole length of the hall, strewn with rich glossy shawls; and on them the merchant kings of those crafty sea-roving Phaeaces sat eating and drinking in pride, and feasting there all the year round. And boys of molten gold stood each on a polished altar, and held torches in their hands, to give light all night to the guests. And round the house sat fifty maid-servants, some grinding the meal in the mill, some turning the spindle, some weaving at the loom, while their hands twinkled as they passed the shuttle, like quivering aspen leaves.

And outside before the palace a great garden was walled round, filled full of stately fruit-trees, grey olives and sweet figs, and pomegranates, pears and apples, which bore the whole year round. For the rich south-west wind fed them till pear grew ripe on pear, fig on fig, and grape on grape, all the winter and the spring. And at the farther end gay flower-beds bloomed through all seasons of the year; and two fair fountains rose and ran, one through the garden grounds, and one beneath the palace gate, to water all the town. Such noble gifts the heavens had given to Alcinous the wise.

So they went in, and saw him sitting, like Poseidon, on his throne, with his golden sceptre by him, in garments stiff with gold, and in his hand a sculptured goblet, as he pledged the merchant kings; and beside him stood Arete, his wise and lovely queen, and leaned against a pillar as she spun her golden threads.

Then Alcinous rose and welcomed them, and bade them sit and eat, and the servants brought them tables, and bread and meat and wine.

But Medeia went trembling toward Arete the fair queen, and fell at her knees and clasped them and cried, weeping as she knelt:

'I am your guest, fair queen, and I entreat you by Zeus, from whom prayers come. Do not send me back to my father to die some dreadful death; but let me go my way, and bear my burden. Have I not had enough of punishment and shame?'

'Who are you, strange maiden? and what is the meaning of your prayer?'

'I am Medeia, daughter of Aietes, and I saw my countrymen here today; and I know that they are come to find me, and take me home to die some dreadful death.'

Then Arete frowned, and said: 'Lead this girl in, my maidens, and let the kings decide, not I.'

And Alcinous leapt up from his throne, and cried: 'Speak, strangers, who are you? And who is this maiden?'

'We are the heroes of the Minyae,' said Jason; 'and this maiden has spoken truth. We are the men who took the golden fleece, the men whose fame has run round every shore. We came hither out of the ocean, after sorrows such as man never saw before. We went out many, and come back few, for many a noble comrade have we lost. So let us go, as you should let your guests go, in peace; that the world may say, "Alcinous is a just king."'

But Alcinous frowned, and stood deep in thought; and at last he spoke:

'Had not the deed been done which is done, I should have said this day to myself, "It is an honour to Alcinous and to his children after him, that the far-famed Argonauts are his guests." But these Colchi are my guests, as you are; and for this month they have waited here with all their fleet, for they have hunted all the seas of Hellas, and could not find you, and dared neither go farther, nor go home.'

'Let them choose out their champions, and we will fight them, man for man.'

'No guests of ours shall fight upon our island, and if you go outside they will outnumber you. I will do justice between you, for I know and do what is right.'

Then he turned to his kings, and said: 'This may stand over till tomorrow. Tonight we will feast our guests, and hear the story of all their wanderings, and how they came hither out of the ocean.'

So Alcinous bade the servants take the heroes in, and bathe them, and give them clothes. And they were glad when they saw the warm water, for it was long since they had bathed. And they washed off the sea-salt from their limbs, and anointed themselves from head to foot with oil, and combed out their golden hair. Then they came back again into the hall, while the merchant kings rose up to do them honour. And each man said to his neighbour: 'No wonder that these men won fame. How they stand now like Giants, or Titans, or Immortals come down from Olympus, though many a winter has worn them, and many a fearful storm. What must they have been when they sailed from Iolcos, in the bloom of their youth, long ago?'

Then they went out to the garden, and the merchant princes said: 'Heroes, run races with us. Let us see whose feet are nimblest.'

'We cannot race against you, for our limbs are stiff from sea, and we have lost our two swift comrades, the sons of the North Wind. But do not think us cowards: if you wish to try our strength, we will shoot and box and wrestle against any men on earth.'

And Alcinous smiled, and answered: 'I believe you, gallant guests; with your long limbs and broad shoulders, we could never match you here. For we care nothing here for boxing, or for shooting with the bow; but for feasts and songs and

harping and dancing and running races to stretch our limbs on shore.'

So they danced there and ran races, the jolly merchant kings, till the night fell, and all went in.

And then they ate and drank and comforted their weary souls, till Alcinous called a herald, and bade him go and fetch the harper.

The herald went out, and fetched the harper and led him in by the hand, and Alcinous cut him a piece of meat from the fattest of the haunch and sent it to him and said: 'Sing to us, noble harper, and rejoice the heroes' hearts.'

So the harper played and sang, while the dancers danced

strange figures; and after that the tumblers showed their tricks, till the heroes laughed again.

Then, 'Tell me, heroes,' asked Alcinous, 'you who have sailed the ocean round, and seen the manners of all nations, have you seen such dancers as ours here, or heard such music and such singing? We hold ours to be the best on earth.'

'Such dancing we have never seen,' said Orpheus, 'and your singer is a happy man, for Phoebus himself must have taught him; or else he is the son of a Muse, as I am also, and have sung once or twice, though not so well as he.'

'Sing to us then, noble stranger,' said Alcinous, 'and we will give you precious gifts.'

So Orpheus took his magic harp and sang to them a stirring song of their voyage from Iolcos, and their dangers, and how they won the golden fleece; and of Medeia's love, and how she helped them, and went with them over land and sea; and of all their fearful dangers, from monsters and rocks and storms, till the heart of Arete was softened, and all the women wept. And the merchant kings rose up, each man from off his golden throne, and clapped their hands, and shouted: 'Hail to the noble Argonauts, who sailed the unknown sea!'

Then he went on and told of their journey over the sluggish northern main, and through the shoreless outer ocean to the fairy island of the west; and of the Sirens, and Scylla and Charybdis, and all the wonders they had seen, till midnight passed and the day dawned; but the kings never thought of sleep. Each man sat still and listened, with his chin upon his hand.

And at last, when Orpheus had ended, they all went thoughtful out, and the heroes lay down to sleep, beneath the sounding

See page 123

HE KILLED THEM ALL WITH HIS POISONED ARROWS

porch outside, where Arete had strewn them rugs and carpets, in the sweet still summer night.

But Arete pleaded hard with her husband for Medeia, for her heart was softened. And she said: 'The gods will punish her, not we. After all, she is our guest and my suppliant, and prayers are the daughters of Zeus. And who, too, dare part man and wife, after all they have endured together?'

And Alcinous smiled. 'The minstrel's song has charmed you; but I must remember what is right, for songs cannot alter justice, and I must be faithful to my name. Alcinous I am called, the man of sturdy sense, and Alcinous I will be.' But for all that Arete besought him, until she won him round.

So next morning he sent a herald, and called the kings into the square, and said: 'This is a puzzling matter . . . remember but one thing: these Minyae live close by us, and we may meet them often on the seas; but Aietes lives afar off, and we have only heard his name. Which then of the two is it safer to offend —the men near us, or the men far off?'

The princes laughed, and praised his wisdom; and Alcinous called the heroes to the square, and the Colchi also; and they came and stood opposite each other, but Medeia stayed in the palace. Then Alcinous spoke: 'Heroes of the Colchi, what is your errand about this lady?'

'To carry her home with us, that she may die a shameful death; but if we return without her, we must die the death she should have died.'

'What say you to this, Jason the Aeolid?' said Alcinous, turning to the Minyae.

'I say', said the cunning Jason, 'that they are come here on a bootless errand. Do you think that you can make her follow you, heroes of the Colchi—her, who knows all spells and charms? She will cast away your ships on quicksands, or call down on you Brimo the wild huntress, or the chains will fall from off her wrists and she will escape in her dragon-car; or if not thus, some other way, for she has a thousand plans and wiles. And why return home at all, brave heroes, and face the long seas again, and the Bosphorus and the stormy Euxine, and double all your toil? There is many a fair land round these coasts which waits for gallant men like you. Better to settle there, and build a city, and let Aietes and Colchis help themselves.'

Then a murmur rose among the Colchi, and some cried: 'He has spoken well,' and some: 'We have had enough of roving; we will sail the seas no more!' And the chief said at last: 'Be it so, then; a plague she has been to us, and a plague to the house of her father, and a plague she will be to you. Take her, since you are no wiser, and we will sail away toward the north.'

Then Alcinous gave them food and water and garments and rich presents of all sorts, and he gave the same to the Minyae and sent them all away in peace.

So Jason kept the dark witch-maiden to breed him woe and shame; and the Colchi went northward into the Adriatic, and settled, and built towns along the shore.

Then the heroes rode away to the eastward, to reach Hellas, their beloved land; but a storm came down upon them, and swept them far away toward the south. And they rowed till they were spent with struggling through the darkness and the blinding rain, but where they were they could not tell, and they gave up all hope of life. And at last they touched the ground, and when daylight came they waded to the shore, and saw nothing round but sand and desolate salt pools, for they had come to the quicksands of the Syrtis and the dreary treeless flats which lie between Numidia and Cyrene, on the burning shore of Africa. And there they wandered starving for many a weary day, ere they could launch their ship again, and gain the open sea. And there Canthus was killed, while he was trying to drive off sheep, by a stone which a herdsman threw.

And there too died Mopsus—the seer who knew the voices of all birds; but he could not foretell his own end, for he was bitten in the foot by a snake, one of those which sprang from the Gorgon's head when Perseus carried it across the sands.

At last they rowed away toward the northward for many a weary day till their water was spent and their food eaten, and they were worn out with hunger and thirst. But at last they saw a long steep island and a blue peak high among the clouds, and they knew it for the peak of Ida and the famous land of Crete. And they said: 'We will land in Crete, and see Minos the just king and all his glory and his wealth; at least he will treat us hospitably, and let us fill our water casks upon the shore.'

But when they came nearer to the island they saw a wondrous sight upon the cliffs. For on a cape to the westward stood a giant, taller than any mountain pine, who glittered aloft against the sky like a tower of burnished brass. He turned and looked on all sides round him, till he saw the *Argo* and her crew; and when he saw them he came toward them, more swiftly than the swiftest horse, leaping across the glens at a bound and striding at one step from down to down. And when he came abreast of them he brandished his arms up and down, as a ship hoists and lowers her yards, and shouted with his brazen throat like a trumpet from off the hills: 'You are pirates, you are robbers! If you dare land here, you die.'

Then the heroes cried: 'We are no pirates. We are all good men and true, and all we ask is food and water'; but the giant cried the more:

'You are robbers, you are pirates all. I know you; and if you land, you shall die the death.'

Then he waved his arms again as a signal, and they saw the people flying inland, driving their flocks before them, while a great flame arose among the hills. Then the giant ran up a valley and vanished, and the heroes lay on their oars in fear.

But Medeia stood watching all from under her steep black brows, with a cunning smile upon her lips, and a cunning plot within her heart. At last she spoke: 'I know this giant. I heard of him in the East. Hephaistos the Fire King made him in his forge in Aetna beneath the earth, and called him Talus, and gave him to Minos for a servant, to guard the coast of Crete. Thrice a day he walks round the island, and never stops to sleep; and if strangers land he leaps into his furnace, which flames there among the hills, and when he is red-hot he rushes on them and burns them in his brazen hands.'

Then all the heroes cried: 'What shall we do, wise Medeia? We must have water or we die of thirst. Flesh and blood we can face fairly, but who can face this red-hot brass?'

'I can face red-hot brass, if the tale I hear be true. For they say that he has but one vein in all his body, filled with liquid fire, and that this vein is closed with a nail: but I know not where that nail is placed. But if I can get it once into these hands, you shall water your ship here in peace.'

Then she bade them put her on shore and row off again and wait what would befall.

And the heroes obeyed her unwillingly, for they were ashamed to leave her so alone; but Jason said: 'She is dearer to me than to any of you, yet I will trust her freely on shore; she has more plots than we can dream of in the windings of that fair and cunning head.'

So they left the witch-maiden on the shore, and she stood there in her beauty all alone, till the giant strode back red-hot from head to heel, while the grass hissed and smoked beneath his tread.

And when he saw the maiden alone, he stopped; and she looked boldly up into his face without moving, and began her magic song:

'Life is short, though life is sweet, and even men of brass and fire must die. The brass must rust, the fire must cool, for time gnaws all things in their turn. Life is short, though life is sweet. But sweeter to live for ever; sweeter to live ever youthful like the gods, who have ichor in their veins— ichor which gives life and youth and joy, and a bounding heart.'

Then Talus said: 'Who are you, strange maiden, and where is this ichor of youth?'

Then Medeia held up a flask of crystal, and said: 'Here is the ichor of youth. I am Medeia the enchantress; my sister Circe gave me this and said: "Go and reward Talus, the faithful servant, for his fame is gone out into all lands." So come, and I will pour this into your veins, that you may live for ever young.'

And he listened to her false words, that simple Talus, and

came near; and Medeia said: 'Dip yourself in the sea first, and cool yourself, lest you burn my tender hands; then show me where the nail in your vein is, that I may pour the ichor in.'

Then that simple Talus dipped himself in the sea, till it hissed, and roared, and smoked; and came and knelt before Medeia, and showed her the secret nail.

And she drew the nail out gently, but she poured no ichor in; and instead the liquid fire spouted forth, like a stream of red-hot iron. And Talus tried to leap up, crying: 'You have betrayed me, false witch-maiden!' But she lifted up her hands before him and sang, till he sank beneath her spell. And as he sank, his brazen limbs clanked heavily, and the earth groaned beneath his weight; and the liquid fire ran from his heel, like a stream of lava, to the sea; and Medeia laughed and called to the heroes: 'Come ashore, and water your ship in peace.'

So they came, and found the giant lying dead; and they fell down and kissed Medeia's feet, and watered their ship, and took sheep and oxen, and so left that inhospitable shore.

At last, after many more adventures, they came to the Cape of Malea, at the south-west point of the Peloponnese. And there they offered sacrifices, and Orpheus purged them from their guilt. Then they rode away again to the northward, past the Laconian shore, and came all worn and tired by Sunium and up the long Euboean Strait, until they saw once more Pelion and Aphetai, and Iolcos by the sea.

And they ran the ship ashore, but they had no strength left to haul her up the beach; and they crawled out on to the pebbles, and sat down, and wept till they could weep no more. For the houses and the trees were all altered, and all the faces which they saw were strange, and their joy was swallowed up in sorrow, while they thought of their youth and all their labour and the gallant comrades they had lost.

And the people crowded round and asked them: 'Who are you, that you sit weeping here?'

'We are the sons of your princes, who sailed out many a year ago. We went to fetch the golden fleece, and we have brought it and grief therewith. Give us news of our fathers and our mothers, if any of them be left alive on earth.'

Then there was shouting and laughing and weeping; and all the kings came to the shore, and they led away the heroes to their homes and bewailed the valiant dead.

Then Jason went up with Medeia to the palace of his uncle Pelias. And when he came in Pelias sat by the hearth, crippled and blind with age, while opposite him sat Aeson, Jason's father, crippled and blind likewise; and the two old men's heads shook together as they tried to warm themselves before the fire.

And Jason fell down at his father's knees and wept, and called him by his name. And the old man stretched out his hands and felt him and said: 'Do not mock me, young hero. My son Jason is dead long ago at sea.'

'I am your own son Jason, whom you trusted to the Centuar upon Pelion; and I have brought home the golden fleece, and a princess of the Sun's race for my bride. So now give me up the kingdom, Pelias my uncle, and fulfil your promise as I have fulfilled mine.'

Then his father clung to him like a child, and wept, and would not let him go; and cried: 'Now I shall not go down lonely to my grave. Promise me never to leave me till I die.'

PART VI

What was the End of the Heroes?

AND now I wish that I could end my story pleasantly, but it is no fault of mine that I cannot. The old songs end it sadly, and I believe that they are right and wise; for though the heroes were purified at Malea, yet sacrifices cannot make bad hearts good, and Jason had taken a wicked wife, and he had to bear his burden to the last.

And first she laid a cunning plot to punish that poor old Pelias, instead of letting him die in peace.

For she told his daughters: 'I can make old things young again. I will show you how easy it is to do.' So she took an old ram and killed him and put him in a cauldron with magic herbs; and whispered her spells over him, and he leapt out again a young lamb. So that 'Medeia's cauldron' is a proverb still, by which we mean times of war and change, when the world has become old and feeble, and grows young again through bitter pains.

Then she said to Pelias' daughters: 'Do to your father as I

did to this ram, and he will grow young and strong again.'
But she told them only half the spell; so they failed, while
Medeia mocked them; and poor old Pelias died, and his
daughters came to misery. But the songs say she cured Aeson,
Jason's father, and he became young and strong again.

But Jason could not love her, after all her cruel deeds. So
he was ungrateful to her, and wronged her, and she revenged
herself on him. And a terrible revenge she took—too terrible
to speak of here. But you will hear of it yourselves when you
grow up, for it has been sung in noble poetry and music. And
whether it be true or not, it stands for ever as a warning to us
not to seek for help from evil persons, or to gain good ends by
evil means. For if we use an adder even against our enemies it
will turn again and sting us.

But of all the other heroes there is many a brave tale left,
which I have no space to tell you, so you must read them for
yourselves: of the hunting of the boar in Calydon, which
Meleager killed; and of Heracles' twelve famous labours; and
of the seven who fought at Thebes; and of the noble love of
Castor and Polydeuces, the twin Dioscouroi—how when one
died the other would not live without him, so they shared
their immortality between them; and Zeus changed them into
the two twin stars which never rise both at once.

And what became of Cheiron, the good immortal beast?
That too is a sad story; for the heroes never saw him more.
He was wounded by a poisoned arrow at Pholoe among the
hills, when Heracles opened the fatal wine jar, which Cheiron
had warned him not to touch. And the Centaurs smelt the
wine and flocked to it and fought for it with Heracles; but he
killed them all with his poisoned arrows and Cheiron was left

alone. Then Cheiron took up one of the arrows and dropped it by chance upon his foot; and the poison ran like fire along his veins, and he lay down and longed to die; and cried: 'Through wine I perish, the bane of all my race. Why should I live for ever in this agony? Who will take my immortality, that I may die?'

Then Prometheus answered, the good Titan, whom Heracles had set free from Caucasus: 'I will take your immortality and live for ever, that I may help poor mortal men.' So Cheiron gave him his immortality and died, and had rest from pain. And Heracles and Prometheus wept over him and went to bury him on Pelion; but Zeus took him up among the stars, to live for ever, grand and mild, low down in the far southern sky.

And in time the heroes died—all but Nestor, the silver-tongued old man—and left behind them valiant sons, but not so great as they had been. Yet their fame, too, lives till this day, for they fought at the ten years' siege of Troy: and their story is in the book which we call Homer, in two of the noblest songs on earth—the *Iliad*, which tells us of the siege of Troy, and Achilles' quarrel with the kings, and the *Odyssey*, which tells the wanderings of Odysseus, through many lands for many years, and how Alcinous sent him home at last, safe to Ithaca, his beloved island, and to Penelope his faithful wife and Telemachus his son and Euphorbus the noble swineherd and the old dog who licked his hand and died. We will read that sweet story, children, by the fire some winter night. And now I will end my tale, and begin another and a more cheerful one, of a hero who became a worthy king and won his people's love.

STORY THREE

Theseus

PART I

How Theseus Lifted the Stone

ONCE upon a time there was a princess in Troezene—Aithra, the daughter of Pittheus the king. She had one fair son named Theseus, the bravest lad in all the land; and Aithra never smiled but when she looked at him, for her husband had forgotten her, and lived far away. And she used to go up to the mountain above Troezene to the temple of Poseidon, and sit there all day looking out across the bay, over Methana to the purple peaks of Aegina and the Attic shore beyond. And when Theseus was full fifteen years old she took him up with her to the temple and into the thickets of the grove which grew in the temple yard. And she led him to a tall plane tree, beneath whose shade grew arbutus, and lentisk, and purple heather bushes. And there she sighed, and said: 'Theseus, my son, go into that thicket, and you will find at the plane tree foot a great flat stone. Lift it, and bring me what lies underneath.'

127

Then Theseus pushed his way in through the thick bushes and saw that they had not been moved for many a year. And searching among their roots he found a great flat stone, all overgrown with ivy and acanthus and moss. He tried to lift it, but he could not. And he tried till the sweat ran down his brow from heat, and the tears from his eyes for shame; but all was of no avail. And at last he came back to his mother, and said: 'I have found the stone, but I cannot lift it; nor do I think that any man could in all Troezene.'

Then she sighed, and said: 'The Gods wait long; but they are just at last. Let it be for another year. The day may come when you will be a stronger man than lives in all Troezene.'

Then she took him by the hand, and went into the temple and prayed, and came down again with Theseus to her home.

And when a full year was past she led Theseus up again to the temple, and bade him lift the stone; but he could not.

Then she sighed, and said the same words again, and went down and came again the next year; but Theseus could not lift the stone then, nor the year after. And he longed to ask his mother the meaning of that stone, and what might lie underneath it; but her face was so sad that he had not the heart to ask.

So he said to himself: 'The day shall surely come when I will lift that stone, though no man in Troezene can.' And in order to grow strong he spent all his days in wrestling and boxing and hurling, and taming horses, and hunting the boar and the bull, and coursing goats and deer among the rocks, till upon all the mountains there was no hunter so swift as Theseus. And he killed Phaia the wild sow of Crommyon, which wasted all the land, till all the people said: 'Surely the gods are with the lad.'

And when his eighteenth year was past Aithra led him up again to the temple, and said: 'Theseus, lift the stone this day, or never know who you are.' And Theseus went into the thicket and stood over the stone and tugged at it, and it moved. Then his spirit swelled within him, and he said: 'If I break my heart in my body, it shall up.' And he tugged at it once more, and lifted it and rolled it over with a shout.

And when he looked beneath it, on the ground lay a sword of bronze with a hilt of glittering gold, and by it a pair of golden sandals; and he caught them up and burst through the bushes like a wild boar and leapt to his mother, holding them high above his head.

But when she saw them she wept long in silence, hiding her fair face in her shawl; and Theseus stood by her wondering, and wept also, he knew not why. And when she was tired of weeping she lifted up her head and laid her finger on her lips and said: 'Hide them in your bosom, Theseus my son, and come with me where we can look down upon the sea.'

Then they went outside the sacred wall and looked down over the bright blue sea, and Aithra said:

'Do you see this land at our feet?'

And he said: 'Yes, this is Troezene, where I was born and bred.'

And she said: 'It is but a little land, barren and rocky, and looks towards the bleak north-east. Do you see that land beyond?'

'Yes, that is Attica, where the Athenian people dwell.'

'That is a fair land and large, Theseus my son, and it looks toward the sunny south—a land of olive oil and honey, the joy of gods and men. For the gods have girdled it with mountains, whose veins are of pure silver, and their bones of marble white as snow; and there the hills are sweet with thyme and basil, and the meadows with violet and asphodel, and the nightingales sing all day in the thickets, by the side of ever-flowing streams. There are twelve towns, well peopled, the homes of an ancient race—the children of Cecrops the serpent-king (the son of Mother Earth) who wear gold cicalas among the tresses of their golden hair; for like the cicalas they sprang from the earth, and like the cicalas they sing all day, rejoicing in the genial sun. What would you do, son Theseus, if you were king of such a land?'

Then Theseus stood astonished, as he looked across the broad bright sea, and saw the fair Attic shore, from Sunium to Hymettus and Pentelicus, and all the mountain peaks which girdle Athens round. But Athens itself he could not see, for purple Aegina stood before it, midway across the sea.

Then his heart grew great within him, and he said: 'If I were king of such a land I would rule it wisely and well in wisdom and in might, that when I died all men might weep over my tomb, and cry: "Alas for the shepherd of his people!"'

And Aithra smiled, and said: 'Take then the sword and the sandals and go to Aegeus, King of Athens, who lives on Pallas' hill; and say to him: "The stone is lifted, but whose is the pledge beneath it?" Then show him the sword and the sandals, and take what the gods shall send.'

But Theseus wept: 'Shall I leave you, O my mother?'

But she answered: 'Weep not for me. That which is fated must be, and grief is easy to those who do nought but grieve.

Full of sorrow was my youth and full of sorrow my woman-hood. Full of sorrow was my youth for Bellerophon, the slayer of the Chimaera, whom my father drove away by treason; and full of sorrow my womanhood for thy treacherous father and for thee, and full of sorrow my old age will be (for I see my fate in dreams) when the sons of the Swan shall carry me captive to the hollow vale of Eurotas, till I sail across the seas a slave, the handmaid of the pest of Greece. Yet shall I be avenged, when the golden-haired heroes sail against Troy, and sack the palaces of Ilium. Then my son shall set me free from thraldom, and I shall hear the tale of Theseus' fame. Yet beyond that I see new sorrows, but I can bear them as I have borne the past.'

Then she kissed Theseus and wept over him, and went into the temple; and Theseus saw her no more.

PART II

How Theseus Slew the Devourers of Men

So Theseus stood there alone, with his mind full of many hopes. And first he thought of going down to the harbour and hiring a swift ship and sailing across the bay to Athens, but even that seemed too slow for him, and he longed for wings to fly across the sea and find his father. But after a while his heart began to fail him; and he sighed, and said within himself:

'What if my father has other sons about him whom he loves? What if he will not receive me? And what have I done that he should receive me? He has forgotten me ever since I was born: why should he welcome me now?'

Then he thought a long while sadly; and at the last he cried aloud: 'Yes, I will make him love me, for I will prove myself worthy of his love. I will win honour and renown and do such deeds that Aegeus shall be proud of me, though he had fifty other sons! Did not Heracles win himself honour, though he was opprest, and the slave of Eurystheus? Did he not kill all robbers and evil beasts, and drain great lakes and marshes, breaking the hills through with his club? Therefore it was that all men honoured him, because he rid them of their miseries and made life pleasant to them and their children after them. Where can I go, to do as Heracles has done? Where can I find strange adventures, robbers, and monsters and the children of hell, the enemies of men? I will go by land and into the mountains and round by the way of the Isthmus. Perhaps there I may hear of brave adventures and do something which shall win my father's love. '

So he went by land and away into the mountains, with his father's sword upon his thigh, till he came to the Spider mountains which hang over Epidaurus and the sea, where the glens run downward from one peak in the midst, as the rays spread in the spider's web.

And he went up into the gloomy glens between the furrowed marble walls till the lowland grew blue beneath his feet and the clouds drove damp about his head.

But he went up and up for ever through the spider's web of glens till he could see the narrow gulfs spread below him, north and south and east and west; black cracks half choked with mists, and above all a dreary down.

But over that down he must go, for there was no road right or left; so he toiled on through bog and brake, till he came to a pile of stones.

And on the stones a man was sitting, wrapt in a bearskin

cloak. The head of the bear served him for a cap, and its teeth grinned white around his brows, and the feet were tied about his throat, and their claws shone white upon his chest. And when he saw Theseus he rose and laughed till the glens rattled.

'And who art thou, fair fly, who hast walked into the spider's web?' But Theseus walked on steadily, and made no answer; but he thought: 'Is this some robber? And has an adventure come already to me?' But the strange man laughed louder than ever, and said:

'Bold fly, know you not that these glens are the web from which no fly ever finds his way out again, and this down the spider's house, and I the spider who sucks the flies? Come hither, and let me feast upon you; for it is of no use to run away, so cunning a web has my father Hephaistos spread for me when he made these clefts in the mountains, through which no man finds his way home.'

But Theseus came on steadily, and asked:

'And what is your name among men, bold spider? And where are your spider's fangs?'

Then the strange man laughed again:

'My name is Periphetes, the son of Hephaistos and Anticleia the mountain nymph. But men call me Corynetes the club-bearer; and here is my spider's fang.'

And he lifted from off the stones at his side a mighty club of bronze.

'This my father gave me and forged it himself in the roots of the mountain; and with it I pound all proud flies till they give out their fatness and their sweetness. So give me up that gay sword of yours and your mantle and your golden sandals, lest I pound you, and by ill luck you die.'

But Theseus wrapt his mantle round his left arm quickly, in hard folds, from his shoulder to his hand, and drew his sword, and rushed upon the club-bearer, and the club-bearer rushed on him.

Thrice he struck at Theseus, and made him bend under the blows like a sapling; but Theseus guarded his head with his left arm, and the mantle which was wrapt around it.

And thrice Theseus sprang upright after the blow, like a sapling when the storm is past; and he stabbed at the club-bearer with his sword, but the loose folds of the bearskin saved him.

Then Theseus grew mad, and closed with him and caught him by the throat, and they fell and rolled over together; but when Theseus rose up from the ground the club-bearer lay still at his feet.

Then Theseus took his club and his bearskin and left him to the kites and crows, and went upon his journey down the glens on the farther slope, till he came to a broad green valley and saw flocks and herds sleeping beneath the trees.

And by the side of a pleasant fountain, under the shade of rocks and trees, were nymphs and shepherds dancing; but no one piped to them while they danced.

And when they saw Theseus they shrieked, and the shepherds ran off, and drove away their flocks, while the nymphs dived into the fountain like coots, and vanished.

Theseus wondered and laughed. 'What strange fancies have folks here who run away from strangers, and have no music when they dance!' But he was tired and dusty and thirsty; so he thought no more of them, but drank and bathed in the clear pool and then lay down in the shade under a plane tree, while the water sang him to sleep, as it tinkled down from stone to stone.

And when he woke he heard a whispering, and saw the nymphs peeping at him across the fountain from the dark mouth of a cave, where they sat on green cushions of moss. And one said: 'Surely he is not Periphetes'; and another: 'He looks like no robber, but a fair and gentle youth.'

Then Theseus smiled and called them. 'Fair nymphs, I am not Periphetes. He sleeps among the kites and crows; but I have brought away his bearskin and his club.'

Then they leapt across the pool and came to him and called the shepherds back. And he told them how he had slain the club-bearer: and the shepherds kissed his feet and sang: 'Now we shall feed our flocks in peace, and not be afraid to have music when we dance; for the cruel club-bearer has met his match, and he will listen for our pipes no more.'

Then they brought him kid's flesh and wine, and the nymphs brought him honey from the rocks, and he ate and drank, and slept again while the nymphs and shepherds danced and sang. And when he woke, they begged him to stay, but he would not. 'I have a great work to do,' he said. 'I must be away toward the Isthmus, that I may go to Athens.'

But the shepherds said: 'Will you go alone toward Athens? None travel that way now, except in armed troops.'

'As for arms, I have enough, as you see. And as for troops, an honest man is good enough company for himself. Why should I not go alone toward Athens?'

'If you do, you must look warily about you on the Isthmus, lest you meet Sinis the robber, whom men call Pituocamptes the pine-bender; for he bends down two pine trees, and binds all travellers hand and foot between them, and when he lets the trees go again their bodies are torn in sunder.'

'And after that', said another, 'you must go inland, and not dare to pass over the cliffs of Sciron; for on the left hand are the mountains, and on the right the sea, so that you have no escape, but must needs meet Sciron the robber, who will make you wash his feet; and while you are washing them he will kick you over the cliff, to the tortoise who lives below, and feeds upon the bodies of the dead.'

And before Theseus could answer, another cried: 'And after that is a worse danger still, unless you go inland always, and leave Eleusis far on your right. For in Eleusis rules Ker-kyon the cruel king, the terror of all mortals, who killed his own daughter Alope in prison. But she was changed into a fair fountain; and her child he cast out upon the mountains, but the wild mares gave it milk. And now he challenges all comers to wrestle with him, for he is the best wrestler in all Attica and overthrows all who come; and those whom he overthrows he murders miserably, and his palace court is full of their bones.'

Then Theseus frowned and said: 'This seems indeed an ill-ruled land, and adventures enough in it to be tried. But if I am the heir of it, I will rule it and right it, and here is my royal sceptre.' And he shook his club of bronze, while the nymphs and shepherds clung around him, and entreated him not to go.

But on he went nevertheless, till he could see both the seas and the citadel of Corinth towering high above all the land. And he passed swiftly along the Isthmus, for his heart burned to meet that cruel Sinis, and in a pine wood at last he met him, where the Isthmus was narrowest and the road ran between high rocks. There he sat upon a stone by the wayside, with a young fir tree for a club across his knees, and a cord laid ready by his side; and over his head, upon the fir tops, hung the bones of murdered men.

Then Theseus shouted to him: 'Holla, thou valiant pine-bender, hast thou two fir trees left for me?'

And Sinis leapt to his feet, and answered, pointing to the bones above his head: 'My larder has grown empty lately, so I have two fir trees ready for thee.' And he rushed on Theseus, lifting his club, and Theseus rushed upon him.

Then they hammered together till the greenwoods rang; but the metal was tougher than the pine, and Sinis' club broke right across, as the bronze came down upon it. Then Theseus heaved up another mighty stroke, and smote Sinis down upon his face, and knelt upon his back and bound him with his own cord and said: 'As thou hast done to others, so shall it be done to thee.' Then he bent down two young fir trees and bound Sinis between them, for all his struggling and his prayers, and let them go, and ended Sinis, and went on, leaving him to the hawks and crows.

Then he went over the hills toward Megara, keeping close along the Saronic Sea, till he came to the cliffs of Sciron, and the narrow path between the mountain and the sea.

And there he saw Sciron sitting by a fountain, at the edge of the cliff. On his knees was a mighty club; and he had barred the path with stones, so that every one must stop who came up.

Then Theseus shouted to him, and said: 'Holla, thou tortoise-feeder, do thy feet need washing today?'

And Sciron leapt to his feet, and answered:

'My tortoise is empty and hungry, and my feet need washing

today.' And he stood before his barrier, and lifted up his club in both hands.

Then Theseus rushed upon him; and sore was the battle upon the cliff, for when Sciron felt the weight of the bronze club, he dropt his own, and closed with Theseus, and tried to hurl him by main force over the cliff. But Theseus was a wary wrestler, and dropt his own club, and caught him by the throat and by the knee, and forced him back against the wall of stones, and crushed him up against them, till his breath was almost gone. And Sciron cried panting: 'Loose me, and I will let thee pass.' But Theseus answered: 'I must not pass till I have made the rough way smooth', and he forced him back against the wall till it fell, and Sciron rolled head over heels.

Then Theseus lifted him up all bruised, and said: 'Come

hither and wash my feet.' And he drew his sword and sat down by the well and said: 'Wash my feet, or I cut you piecemeal.'

And Sciron washed his feet trembling, and when it was done Theseus rose and cried, 'As thou hast done to others, so shall it be done to thee. Go feed thy tortoise thyself'; and he kicked him over the cliff into the sea.

And whether the tortoise ate him, I know not; for some say that earth and sea both disdained to take his body, so foul it was with sin. So the sea cast it out upon the shore and the shore cast it back into the sea, and at last the waves hurled it high into the air in anger, and it hung there long without a grave till it was changed into a desolate rock, which stands there in the surge until this day.

This at least is true, which Pausanias tells, that in the royal porch at Athens he saw the figure of Theseus modelled in clay, and by him Sciron the robber falling headlong into the sea.

Then he went a long day's journey past Megara into the Attic land, and high before him rose the snow peaks of Cithaeron, all cold above the black pine woods, where haunt the Furies, and the raving Bacchae, and the nymphs who drive men wild, far aloft upon the dreary mountains, where the storms howl all day long. And on his right hand was the sea always and Salamis, with its island cliffs, and the sacred strait of the sea fight, where afterwards the Persians fled before the Greeks. So he went all day until the evening, till he saw the Thriasian plain, and the sacred city of Eleusis, where the Earth-mother's temple stands. For there she met Triptolemus, when all the land lay waste, Demeter the kind Earth-mother, and in her hands a sheaf of corn. And she taught him to plough the fallows, and to yoke the lazy kine; and she taught him to sow

the seed-fields, and to reap the golden grain, and sent him forth
to teach all nations and give corn to labouring men. So at
Eleusis all men honour her, whosoever tills the land, her and
Triptolemus her beloved who gave corn to labouring men.

And he went along the plain into Eleusis, and stood in the
market-place, and cried:

'Where is Kerkyon, the king of the city? I must wrestle a
fall with him today.'

Then all the people crowded round him, and cried: 'Fair
youth, why will you die? Hasten out of the city, before the
cruel king hears that a stranger is here.'

But Theseus went up through the town, while the people
wept and prayed, and through the gates of the palace yard,
and through the piles of bones and skulls, till he came to the
door of Kerkyon's hall, the terror of all mortal men.

And there he saw Kerkyon sitting at the table in the hall
alone; and before him was a whole sheep roasted, and beside
him a whole jar of wine. And Theseus stood and called him:
'Holla, thou valiant wrestler, wilt thou wrestle a fall today?'

And Kerkyon looked up and laughed, and answered: 'I
will wrestle a fall today, but come in, for I am lonely and thou
weary, and eat and drink before thou die.'

Then Theseus went up boldly, and sat down before Kerkyon
at the board, and he ate his fill of the sheep's flesh, and drank
his fill of the wine; and Theseus ate enough for three men, but
Kerkyon ate enough for seven.

But neither spoke a word to the other, though they looked
across the table by stealth; and each said in his heart: 'He has
broad shoulders: but I trust mine are as broad as his.'

At last, when the sheep was eaten and the jar of wine drained dry, King Kerkyon rose, and cried: 'Let us wrestle a fall before we sleep.'

So they tossed off all their garments and went forth in the palace yard; and Kerkyon bade strew fresh sand in an open space between the bones. And there the heroes stood face to face, while their eyes glared like wild bulls'; and all the people crowded at the gates to see what would befall.

And there they stood and wrestled, till the stars shone out above their heads; up and down and round, till the sand was stamped hard beneath their feet. And their eyes flashed like stars in the darkness and their breath went up like smoke in the night air; but neither took nor gave a footstep, and the people watched silent at the gates.

But at last Kerkyon grew angry and caught Theseus round the neck and shook him as a mastiff shakes a rat; but he could not shake him off his feet.

But Theseus was quick and wary, and clasped Kerkyon round the waist, and slipped his loin quickly underneath him, while he caught him by the wrist; and then he hove a mighty heave, a heave which would have stirred an oak, and lifted Kerkyon, and pitched him right over his shoulder on to the ground.

Then he leapt on him, and called: 'Yield, or I kill thee!' but Kerkyon said no word; for his heart was burst within him with the fall and the meat and the wine.

Then Theseus opened the gates and called in all the people; and they cried: 'You have slain our evil king; be you now our king and rule us well.'

'I will be your king in Eleusis and I will rule you right and well; for this cause I have slain all evildoers—Sinis and Sciron, and this man last of all.'

Then an aged man stepped forth, and said: 'Young hero, hast thou slain Sinis? Beware then of Aegeus, King of Athens, to whom thou goest, for he is near of kin to Sinis.'

'Then I have slain my own kinsman,' said Theseus, 'though well he deserved to die. Who will purge me from his death, for rightfully I slew him, unrighteous and accursed as he was?'

And the old man answered:

'That will the heroes do, the sons of Phytalus, who dwell beneath the elm tree in Aphidnai, by the bank of silver Cephisus; for they know the mysteries of the gods. Thither you shall go and be purified, and after you shall be our king.'

So he took an oath of the people of Eleusis, that they would serve him as their king, and went away next morning across the Thriasian plain, and over the hills toward Aphidnai, that he might find the sons of Phytalus.

And as he was skirting the Vale of Cephisus along the foot of lofty Parnes, a very tall and strong man came down to meet him, dressed in rich garments. On his arms were golden bracelets and round his neck a collar of jewels; and he came forward, bowing courteously, and held out both his hands, and spoke:

'Welcome, fair youth, to these mountains; happy am I to have met you! For what greater pleasure to a good man than to entertain strangers? But I see that you are weary. Come up to my castle, and rest yourself awhile.'

'I give you thanks,' said Theseus, 'but I am in haste to go up the valley, and to reach Aphidnai in the Vale of Cephisus.'

'Alas! you have wandered far from the right way, and you cannot reach Aphidnai tonight, for there are many miles of mountain between you and it, and steep passes and cliffs dangerous after nightfall. It is well for you that I met you, for

my whole joy is to find strangers, and to feast them at my castle'
and hear tales from them of foreign lands. Come up with me,
and eat the best of venison and drink the rich red wine, and
sleep upon my famous bed, of which all travellers say that they
never saw the like. For whatsoever the stature of my guest,
however tall or short, that bed fits him to a hair, and he sleeps
on it as he never slept before.' And he laid hold on Theseus'
hands, and would not let him go.

Theseus wished to go forward, but he was ashamed to seem
churlish to so hospitable a man, and he was curious to see that
wondrous bed; and beside, he was hungry and weary. Yet he
shrank from the man, he knew not why; for though his voice
was gentle and fawning it was dry and husky like a toad's;
and though his eyes were gentle, they were dull and cold like
stones. But he consented, and went with the man up a glen
which led from the road toward the peaks of Parnes, under the
dark shadow of the cliffs.

And as they went up, the glen grew narrower and the cliffs
higher and darker, and beneath them a torrent roared, half seen
between bare limestone crags. And around them was neither
tree nor bush, while from the white peaks of Parnes the snow-
blasts swept down the glen, cutting and chilling, till a horror
fell on Theseus as he looked round at that doleful place. And
he asked at last: 'Your castle stands, it seems, in a dreary
region.'

'Yes; but once within it, hospitality makes all things
cheerful. But who are these?' and he looked back, and Theseus
also, and far below along the road which they had left came a
string of laden asses, and merchants walking by them, watching
their ware.

'Ah, poor souls!' said the stranger. 'Well for them that I looked back and saw them! And well for me too, for I shall have the more guests at my feast. Wait awhile till I go down and call them, and we will eat and drink together the livelong night. Happy am I, to whom Heaven sends so many guests at once!'

And he ran back down the hill, waving his hand and shouting to the merchants, while Theseus went slowly up the steep pass.

But as he went up he met an aged man, who had been gathering driftwood in the torrent bed. He had laid down his faggot in the road and was trying to lift it again to his shoulder. And when he saw Theseus, he called to him, and said:

'Oh fair youth, help me up with my burden, for my limbs are stiff and weak with years.'

Then Theseus lifted the burden on his back. And the old man blest him, and then looked earnestly upon him and said:

'Who are you, fair youth, and wherefore travel you this doleful road?'

'Who I am my parents know; but I travel this doleful road

because I have been invited by a hospitable man, who promises to feast me, and to make me sleep upon I know not what wondrous bed.'

Then the old man clapped his hands together and cried:

'Oh house of Hades, man-devouring! Will thy maw never be full? Know, fair youth, that you are going to torment and to death, for he who met you (I will requite your kindness by another) is a robber and a murderer of men. Whatsoever stranger he meets he entices him hither to death; and as for this bed of which he speaks, truly it fits all comers, yet none ever rose alive off it save me.'

'Why?' asked Theseus, astonished.

'Because, if a man be too tall for it, he lops his limbs till they be short enough, and if he be too short, he stretches his limbs till they be long enough; but me only he spared, seven weary years agone, for I alone of all fitted his bed exactly, so he spared me and made me his slave. And once I was a wealthy merchant and dwelt in brazen-gated Thebes; but now I hew wood and draw water for him, the torment of all mortal men.'

Then Theseus said nothing, but he ground his teeth together.

'Escape, then,' said the old man, 'for he will have no pity on thy youth. But yesterday he brought up hither a young man and a maiden, and fitted them upon his bed; and the young man's hands and feet he cut off, but the maiden's limbs he stretched until she died, and so both perished miserably—but I am tired of weeping over the slain. And therefore he is called Procrustes the stretcher, though his father called him Damastes. Flee from him: yet whither will you flee? The cliffs are steep, and who can climb them? And there is no other road.'

But Theseus laid his hand upon the old man's mouth, and said: 'There is no need to flee,' and he turned to go down the pass.

'Do not tell him that I have warned you, or he will kill me by some evil death'; and the old man screamed after him down the glen, but Theseus strode on in his wrath.

And he said to himself: 'This is an ill-ruled land: when shall I have done ridding it of monsters?' And as he spoke, Procrustes came up the hill and all the merchants with him, smiling and talking gaily. And when he saw Theseus, he cried: 'Ah, fair young guest, have I kept you too long waiting?'

But Theseus answered: 'The man who stretches his guests upon a bed and hews off their hands and feet, what shall be done to him, when right is done throughout the land?'

Then Procrustes' countenance changed, and his cheeks grew as green as a lizard, and he felt for his sword in haste; but Theseus leapt on him, and cried:

'Is this true, my host, or is it false?' and he clasped Procrustes round waist and elbow, so that he could not draw his sword. 'Is this true, my host, or is it false?'

But Procrustes answered never a word.

Then Theseus flung him from him, and lifted up his dreadful club, and before Procrustes could strike him he had struck and felled him to the ground.

And once again he struck him, and his evil soul fled forth and went down to Hades, squeaking like a bat into the darkness of a cave.

Then Theseus stript him of his gold ornaments and went up to his house, and found there great wealth and treasure, which he had stolen from the passers by. And he called the people of the country, whom Procrustes had despoiled a long time, and parted the spoil among them, and went down the mountains, and away.

And he went down the glens of Parnes, through mist and cloud and rain, down the slopes of oak and lentisk and arbutus and fragrant bay, till he came to the Vale of Cephisus, and the pleasant town of Aphidnai, and the home of the Phytalid heroes, where they dwelt beneath a mighty elm.

And there they built an altar, and bade him bathe in Cephisus and offer a yearling ram, and purified him from the blood of Sinis and sent him away in peace.

And he went down the valley by Acharnai, and by the silver-swirling stream—while all the people blessed him, for the fame of his prowess had spread wide—till he saw the plain of Athens and the hill where Athené dwells.

So Theseus went up through Athens, and all the people ran out to see him; for his fame had gone before him, and every one knew of his mighty deeds. And all cried: 'Here comes the hero who slew Sinis and Phaia the wild sow of Crommyon, and conquered Kerkyon in wrestling and slew Procrustes the pitiless.' But Theseus went on sadly and steadfastly, for his heart yearned after his father, and he said: 'How shall I deliver him from these leeches who suck his blood?'

So he went up the holy stairs, and into the Acropolis, where Aegeus' palace stood; and he went straight into Aegeus' hall and stood upon the threshold and looked round.

And there he saw his cousins sitting about the table at the wine, many a son of Pallas, but no Aegeus among them. There they sat and feasted and laughed and passed the winecup round, while harpers harped, and slave-girls sang, and the tumblers showed their tricks.

Loud laughed the sons of Pallas, and fast went the wine-cup round; but Theseus frowned, and said under his breath: 'No wonder that the land is full of robbers, while such as these bear rule.'

Then the Pallantids saw him, and called to him, half drunk with wine: 'Holla, tall stranger at the door, what is your will today?'

'I come hither to ask for hospitality.'

'Then take it, and welcome. You look like a hero and a bold warrior, and we like such to drink with us.'

'I ask no hospitality of you: I ask it of Aegeus the king, the master of this house.'

At that some growled, and some laughed, and shouted: 'Heyday! We are all masters here.'

'Then I am master as much as the rest of you,' said Theseus; and he strode past the table up the hall, and looked around for Aegeus, but he was nowhere to be seen.

The Pallantids looked at him, and then at each other; and each whispered to the man next him: 'This is a forward fellow; he ought to be thrust out at the door.' But each man's neighbour whispered in return: 'His shoulders are broad; will you rise and put him out?' So they all sat still where they were.

Then Theseus called to the servants, and said: 'Go tell King Aegeus, your master, that Theseus of Troezene is here, and asks to be his guest awhile.'

A servant ran and told Aegeus, where he sat in his chamber within, by Medeia the dark witch-woman, watching her eye and hand. And when Aegeus heard of Troezene he turned pale and red again, and rose from his seat trembling, while Medeia watched him like a snake.

'What is Troezene to you?' she asked. But he said hastily: 'Do you not know who this Theseus is? The hero who has cleared the country from all monsters; but that he came from Troezene, I never heard before. I must go out and welcome him.'

So Aegeus came out into the hall, and when Theseus saw him, his heart leapt into his mouth, and he longed to fall on his neck and welcome him; but he controlled himself, and said: 'My father may not wish for me, after all. I will try him before I discover myself'; and he bowed low before Aegeus, and said: 'I have delivered the king's realm from many monsters; therefore I am come to ask a reward of the king.'

And old Aegeus looked on him, and loved him, as what fond heart would not have done? But he only sighed, and said:

'It is little that I can give you, noble lad, and nothing that is worthy of you; for surely you are no mortal man, or at least no mortal's son.'

'All I ask', said Theseus, 'is to eat and drink at your table.'

'That I can give you,' said Aegeus, 'if at least I am master in my own hall.'

Then he bade them put a seat for Theseus, and set before him the best of the feast; and Theseus sat and ate so much that all the company wondered at him; but always he kept his club by his side.

But Medeia the dark witch-woman had been watching him all the while. She saw how Aegeus turned red and pale when the lad said that he came from Troezene. She saw too how his heart was opened toward Theseus; and how Theseus bore himself before all the sons of Pallas like a lion among a pack of curs. And she said to herself: 'This youth will be master here; perhaps he is nearer to Aegeus already than mere fancy. At least the Pallantids will have no chance by the side of such as he.'

Then she went back into her chamber modestly while Theseus ate and drank; and all the servants whispered: 'This then is the man who killed the monsters! How noble are his looks and how huge his size! Ah, would that he were our master's son!'

But presently Medeia came forth, decked in all her jewels and her rich Eastern robes, and looking more beautiful than the day, so that all the guests could look at nothing else. And in her right hand she held a golden cup, and in her left a flask of gold; and she came up to Theseus and spoke in a sweet, soft, winning voice:

'Hail to the hero, the conqueror, the unconquered, the destroyer of evil things! Drink, hero, of my charmed cup which gives rest after every toil, which heals all wounds and pours new life into the veins. Drink of my cup, for in it sparkles the wine of the east, and Nepenthe, the comfort of the Immortals.'

And as she spoke, she poured the flask into the cup, and the fragrance of the wine spread through the hall, like the scent of thyme and roses.

And Theseus looked up in her fair face and into her deep dark eyes. And as he looked, he shrank and shuddered; for they were dry like the eyes of a snake. And he rose, and said: 'The wine is rich and fragrant, and the wine-bearer as fair as the Immortals; but let her pledge me first herself in the cup, that the wine may be the sweeter from her lips.'

Then Medeia turned pale, and stammered: 'Forgive me, fair hero, but I am ill, and dare drink no wine.'

And Theseus looked again into her eyes, and cried: 'Thou shalt pledge me in that cup, or die.' And he lifted up his brazen club, while all the guests looked on aghast.

Medeia shrieked a fearful shriek, and dashed the cup to the ground, and fled; and where the wine flowed over the marble

pavement, the stone bubbled, and crumbled, and hissed, under the fierce venom of the draught.

But Medeia called her dragon chariot, and sprang into it and fled aloft away over land and sea and no man saw her more.

And Aegeus cried: 'What hast thou done?' But Theseus pointed to the stone. 'I have rid the land of an enchantment; now I will rid it of one more.'

And he came close to Aegeus, and drew from his bosom the sword and the sandals, and said the words which his mother bade him.

And Aegeus stepped back a pace, and looked at the lad till his eyes grew dim; and then he cast himself on his neck and wept, and Theseus wept on his neck, till they had no strength left to weep more.

Then Aegeus turned to all the people, and cried: 'Behold my son, children of Cecrops, a better man than his father was before him.'

Who then were mad but the Pallantids, though they had been mad enough before? And one shouted: 'Shall we make room for an upstart, a pretender, who comes from we know not where?' And another: 'If he be one, we are more than one, and the stronger can hold his own.' And one shouted one thing, and one another; for they were hot and wild with wine; but all caught swords and lances off the wall, where the weapons hung around, and sprang forward to Theseus, and Theseus sprang forward to them.

And he cried: 'Go in peace, if you will, my cousins; but if not, your blood be on your own heads.' But they rushed at him; and then stopped short and railed him, as curs stop and bark when they rouse a lion from his lair.

But one hurled a lance from the rear rank, which passed close by Theseus' head, and at that Theseus rushed forward, and the fight began indeed. Fifty against one they fought, and yet Theseus beat them all; and those who were left fled down into the town, where the people set on them, and drove them out, till Theseus was left alone in the palace, with Aegeus his new-found father. But before nightfall all the town came up with victims, and dances and songs, and they offered sacrifices to Athené and rejoiced all the night long, because their king had found a noble son, and an heir to his royal house.

So Theseus stayed with his father all the winter, and when the spring equinox drew near, all the Athenians grew sad and silent, and Theseus saw it, and asked the reason; but no one would answer him a word.

Then he went to his father, and asked him: but Aegeus turned away his face and wept.

'Do not ask, my son, beforehand, about evils which must happen: it is enough to have to face them when they come.'

And when the spring equinox came a herald came to Athens, and stood in the market, and cried: 'O people and King of Athens, where is your yearly tribute?' Then a great lamentation arose throughout the city. But Theseus stood up to the herald, and cried:

'And who are you, dog-faced, who dare demand tribute here? If I did not reverence your herald's staff, I would brain you with this club.'

And the herald answered proudly, for he was a grave and ancient man:

'Fair youth, I am not dog-faced or shameless; but I do my master's bidding, Minos, the King of hundred-citied Crete, the wisest of all kings on earth. And you must surely be a stranger here, or you would know why I come, and that I come by right.'

'I am a stranger here. Tell me then why you come.'

'To fetch the tribute which King Aegeus promised to Minos, and confirmed his promise with an oath. For Minos conquered all this land, and Megara which lies to the west, when he came hither with a great fleet of ships, enraged about the murder of his son. For his son Androgeos came hither to the Panathenaic games, and overcame all the Greeks in the sports, so that the people honoured him as a hero. But when Aegeus saw his valour, he envied him, and feared lest he should join the sons of Pallas, and take away the sceptre from him. So he plotted against his life, and slew him basely, no man knows how or where. Some say that he waylaid him by Oinoe, on the road which goes to Thebes, and some that he sent him against the bull of Marathon, that the beast might kill him. But Aegeus says that the young men killed him from envy, because he had conquered them in the games. So Minos came hither and avenged him, and would not depart till this land had promised him tribute—seven youths and seven maidens every year, who go with me in a black-sailed ship, till they come to hundred-citied Crete.'

And Theseus ground his teeth together, and said: 'Wert thou not a herald I would kill thee for saying such things of my father; but I will go to him, and know the truth.' So he went to his father, and asked him, but he turned away his head and wept, and said: 'Blood was shed in the land unjustly, and by blood it is avenged. Break not my heart by question; it is enough to endure in silence.'

Then Theseus groaned inwardly, and said: 'I will go myself with these youths and maidens, and kill Minos upon his royal throne.'

And Aegeus shrieked and cried: 'You shall not go, my son, the light of my old age, to whom alone I look to rule this people after I am dead and gone. You shall not go, to die horribly, as those youths and maidens die; for Minos thrusts them into a labyrinth, which Daidalos made for him among the rocks—Daidalos the renegade, the accursed, the pest of this his native land. From that labyrinth no one can escape, entangled in its winding ways, before they meet the Minotaur, the monster who feeds upon the flesh of men. There he devours them horribly, and they never see this land again.'

Then Theseus grew red and his ears tingled and his heart beat loud in his bosom. And he stood awhile like a tall stone pillar on the cliffs above some hero's grave, and at last he spoke:

'Therefore all the more I will go with them, and slay the accursed beast. Have I not slain all evil-doers and monsters, that I might free this land? Where are Periphetes, and Sinis and Kerkyon and Phaia the wild sow? Where are the fifty sons of Pallas? And this Minotaur shall go the road which they have gone, and Minos himself, if he dare stay me.'

'But how will you slay him, my son? For you must leave your club and your armour behind, and be cast to the monster, defenceless and naked like the rest.'

And Theseus said: 'Are there no stones in that labyrinth; and have I not fists and teeth? Did I need my club to kill Kerkyon, the terror of all mortal men?'

Then Aegeus clung to his knees, but he would not hear; and at last he let him go, weeping bitterly, and said only this one word:

'Promise me but this, if you return in peace, though that may hardly be: take down the black sail of the ship (for I shall watch for it all day upon the cliffs) and hoist instead a white sail; that I may know afar off that you are safe.'

And Theseus promised and went out and to the market-place where the herald stood, while they drew lots for the youths and maidens, who were to sail in that doleful crew. And the people stood wailing and weeping, as the lot fell on this one and on that; but Theseus strode into the midst, and cried:

'Here is a youth who needs no lot. I myself will be one of the seven.'

And the herald asked in wonder: 'Fair youth, know you whither you are going?'

And Theseus said: 'I know. Let us go down to the black-sailed ship.'

So they went down to the black-sailed ship, seven maidens and seven youths and Theseus before them all, and the people following them lamenting. But Theseus whispered to his companions: 'Have hope, for the monster is not immortal. Where are Periphetes and Sinis and Sciron and all whom I have slain?' Then their hearts were comforted a little, but they wept as they went on board, and the cliffs of Sunium rang, and all the isles of the Aegean Sea with the voice of their lamentation, as they sailed on towards their deaths in Crete.

PART III

How Theseus Slew the Minotaur

AND at last they came to Crete, and to Cnossus, beneath the peaks of Ida, and to the palace of Minos, the great king, to whom Zeus himself taught laws. So he was the wisest of all mortal kings, and conquered all the Aegean isles, and his ships were as many as the sea-gulls, and his palace like a marble hill. And he sat among the pillars of the hall, upon his throne of beaten gold, and around him stood the speaking statues which Daidalos had made by his skill. For Daidalos was the most cunning of all Athenians, and he invented the plumb-line and the auger and glue, and many a tool with which wood is wrought. And he first set up masts in ships, and yards, and his son made sails for them; but Perdix his nephew excelled him, for he invented the saw and its teeth, copying it from the backbone of a fish, and invented, too, the chisel and the compasses, and the potter's wheel which moulds the clay. Therefore Daidalos envied him, and hurled him headlong from the temple of Athené; but the goddess pitied him (for she loves the wise) and changed him into a partridge, which flits for ever about the hills. And Daidalos fled to Crete, to Minos, and worked for him many a year, till he did a shameful deed, at which the sun hid his face on high.

Then he fled from the anger of Minos, he and Icaros his son having made themselves wings of feathers, and fixed the feathers with wax. So they flew over the sea towards Sicily; but Icaros flew too near the sun; and the wax of his wings was melted, and he fell into the Icarian Sea. But Daidalos came safe to Sicily, and there wrought many a wondrous work, for he made for King Cocalos a reservoir, from which a great river watered all the land, and a castle and a treasury on a mountain, which the giants themselves could not have stormed. And in Selinos he took the steam which comes up from the fires of Aetna, and made of it a warm bath of vapour, to cure the pains of mortal men, and he made a honeycomb of gold, in which the bees came and stored their honey, and in Egypt he made the forecourt of the temple of Hephaistos in Memphis, and a statue of himself within it, and many another wondrous work. And for Minos he made statues which spoke and moved, and the temple of Britomartis, and the dancing-hall of Ariadne, which he carved of fair white stone. And in Sardinia he worked for Iölaos, and in many a land beside, wandering up and down for ever with his cunning, unlovely and accursed by men.

But Theseus stood before Minos, and they looked each other in the face. And Minos bade take them to prison, and cast them to the monster one by one, that the death of Androgeos might be avenged. Then Theseus cried:

'A boon, O Minos! Let me be thrown first to the beast. For I came hither for that very purpose of my own will, and not by lot.'

'Who art thou, then, brave youth?'

'I am the son of him whom of all men thou hatest most —Aegeus the King of Athens; and I am come here to end this matter.'

And Minos pondered awhile, looking steadfastly at him, and he thought: 'The lad means to atone by his own death for his father's sin'; and he answered at last mildly:

'Go back in peace, my son. It is a pity that one so brave should die.'

But Theseus said: 'I have sworn that I will not go back till I have seen the monster face to face.'

And at that Minos frowned, and said: 'Then thou shalt see him; take the madman away.'

And they led Theseus away into the prison, with the other youths and maids.

But Ariadne, Minos' daughter, saw him, as she came out of her white stone hall; and she loved him for his courage and his majesty, and said: 'Shame that such a youth should die!' And by night she went down to the prison, and told him all her heart, and said:

'Flee down to your ship at once, for I have bribed the guards before the door. Flee, you and all your friends, and go back in peace to Greece, and take me, take me with you! For I dare not stay after you are gone, for my father will kill me miserably, if he knows what I have done.'

And Theseus stood silent awhile, for he was astonished and confounded by her beauty; but at last he said: 'I cannot go home in peace, till I have seen and slain this Minotaur, and avenged the deaths of the youths and maidens and put an end to the terrors of my land.'

'And will you kill the Minotaur? How, then?'

'I know not, nor do I care: but he must be strong, if he be too strong for me.'

Then she loved him all the more, and said:

'But when you have killed him, how will you find your way out of the labyrinth?'

'I know not, neither do I care: but it must be a strange road, if I do not find it out before I have eaten up the monster's carcass.'

Then she loved him all the more, and said:

'Fair youth, you are too bold; but I can help you, weak as I am. I will give you a sword, and with that perhaps you may slay the beast; and a clue of thread, and by that, perhaps, you may find your way out again. Only promise me that if you escape safe you will take me home with you to Greece, for my father will surely kill me, if he knows what I have done.'

Then Theseus laughed and said: 'Am I not safe enough now?' And he hid the sword in his bosom, and rolled up the clue in his hand, and then he swore to Ariadne, and fell down before her and kissed her hands and her feet, and she wept over him a long while, and then went away; and Theseus lay down and slept sweetly.

And when the evening came, the guards came in and led him away to the labyrinth.

And he went down into that doleful gulf, through winding paths among the rocks, under caverns and arches and galleries and over heaps of fallen stone. And he turned on the left hand and on the right hand, and went up and down, till his head was dizzy; but all the while he held his clue. For when he went in he had fastened it to a stone, and left it to unroll out of his hand as he went on; and it lasted him till he met the Minotaur, in a narrow chasm between black cliffs.

And when he saw him he stopped awhile, for he had never seen so strange a beast. His body was a man's; but his head was the head of a bull, and his teeth were the teeth of a lion, and with them he tore his prey. And when he saw Theseus he roared, and put his head down, and rushed right at him.

But Theseus stept aside nimbly, and as he passed by, cut him in the knee; and ere he could turn in the narrow path, he followed him, and stabbed him again and again from behind, till the monster fled bellowing wildly; for never before had he felt a wound. And Theseus followed him at full speed, holding the clue of thread in his left hand.

Then on, through cavern after cavern, under dark ribs of sounding stone, and up rough glens and torrent beds, among the sunless roots of Ida, and to the edge of the eternal snow, went they, the hunter and the hunted, while the hills bellowed to the monster's bellow.

And at last Theseus came up with him, where he lay panting on a slab among the snow, and caught him by the horns, and forced his head back and drove the keen sword through his throat.

Then he turned, and went back limping and weary, feeling his way down by the clue of thread, till he came to the mouth of that doleful place; and saw waiting for him—whom but Ariadne!

And he whispered: 'It is done!' and showed her the sword; and she laid her finger on her lips and led him to the prison, and opened the doors, and set all the prisoners free, while the guards lay sleeping heavily, for she had silenced them with wine.

Then they fled to their ship together and leapt on board and hoisted up the sail; and the night lay dark around them, so that they passed through Minos' ships and escaped all safe to Naxos; and there Ariadne became Theseus' wife.

PART IV

How Theseus Fell by his Pride

BUT that fair Ariadne never came to Athens with her husband. Some say that Theseus left her sleeping on Naxos among the Cyclades, and that Dionysos the wine-king found her, and took her up into the sky, as you shall see some day in a painting of old Titian's—one of the most glorious pictures upon earth. And some say that Dionysos drove away Theseus, and took Ariadne from him by force; but however that may be, in his haste or in his grief, Theseus forgot to put up the white sail. Now Aegeus his father sat and watched on Sunium day after day, and strained his old eyes across the sea to see the ship afar. And when he saw the black sail, and not the white one, he gave up Theseus for dead, and in his grief he fell into the sea, and died; so it is called the Aegean to this day.

And now Theseus was King of Athens, and he guarded it and ruled it well.

For he killed the bull of Marathon, which had killed Androgeos, Minos' son; and he drove back the famous Amazons, the
warlike women of the East, when they came from Asia and
conquered all Hellas, and broke into Athens itself. But Theseus
stopped them there and conquered them, and took Hippolyte
their queen to be his wife. Then he went out to fight against
the Lapithai, and Peirithoos their famous king; but when the
two heroes came face to face they loved each other and
embraced and became noble friends; so that the friendship of
Theseus and Peirithoos is a proverb even now. And he gathered
(so the Athenians say) all the boroughs of the land together
and knit them into one strong people, while before they were
all parted and weak: and many another wise thing he did, so
that his people honoured him after he was dead, for many a
hundred years, as the father of their freedom and their laws.
And six hundred years after his death, in the famous fight at
Marathon, men said that they saw the ghost of Theseus, with
his mighty brazen club, fighting in the van of battle against
the invading Persians, for the country which he loved. And
twenty years after Marathon his bones (they say) were found
in Scyros, an isle beyond the sea; and they were bigger than the
bones of mortal man. So the Athenians brought them home in
triumph, and all the people came out to welcome them, and
they built over them a noble temple and adorned it with
sculptures and paintings; in which we are told all the noble
deeds of Theseus and the Centaurs, and the Lapithai and the
Amazons; and the ruins of it are standing still.

But why did they find his bones in Scyros? Why did he not
die in peace at Athens, and sleep by his father's side? Because
after his triumph he grew proud, and broke the laws of God

and man. And one thing worst of all he did, which brought
him to his grave with sorrow. For he went down (they say
beneath the earth) with that bold Peirithoos his friend to help
him to carry off Persephone the queen of the world below.
But Peirithoos was killed miserably, in the dark fire kingdoms
underground; and Theseus was chained to a rock in everlasting
pain. And there he sat for years, till Heracles the mighty came
down to bring up the three-headed dog who sits at Pluto's
gate. So Heracles loosed him from his chains, and brought him
up to the light once more.

But when he came back his people had forgotten him, and
Castor and Polydeuces, the sons of the wondrous Swan, had
invaded his land and carried off his mother Aithra for a slave,
in revenge for a grievous wrong.

So the fair land of Athens was wasted, and another king ruled
it, who drove out Theseus shamefully, and he fled across the
sea to Scyros. And there he lived in sadness, in the house of
Lycomedes the king, till Lycomedes killed him by treachery,
and there was an end of all his labours.

So it is still, my children, and so it will be to the end. In
those old Greeks, and in us also, all strength and virtue come
from God. But if men grow proud and self-willed, and misuse
God's fair gifts, He lets them go their own ways, and fall
pitifully, that the glory may be His alone. God help us all and
give us wisdom and courage to do noble deeds! But God keep
pride from us when we have done them, lest we fall and come
to shame!

The Twelve Labours of Heracles

by Grace Rhys

IT IS an enchanted world that this book of heroes leads us into, almost a fairy world, but not quite, because it is more fresh and daylight than fairy worlds are apt to be. When we look back into the far past to discover the early world of the Greek heroes, it is not into the darkness we have to look, but into a bright land where the sun shines much and often, where the meadows are green and sprinkled with flowers, where the small shining rivers flow merrily down to the sea, and the beautiful mountains rise up into the violet sky. This lovely land is set in the Mediterranean Sea, or 'the Sea of the Middle of the Earth'. From east and west and south the travellers come to the wonderful harbours of Greece that wind so securely in from the sea. All these travellers' tales of the splendid East this wise and simple people hearken to and are made wiser by, till at last they themselves build up a state which, though so small, is nobler and greater than any that are to be found in the East.

In the days of the first heroes, the towns are very small and closely walled about: the people all through the land are full

of fancies and are great weavers of tales. There is no end to the
wonders that surround them. Every forest tree has its nymph,
that makes her home within it and sometimes looks out from
among the branches or wanders along the forest paths, fleeing
back to her shelter the moment a strange foot is heard. Every
river has its water spirit that comes leaping cheerily down from
the mountains and runs with the ripples on their way to the
sea. The rainbow is Iris, a fair maiden, the messenger between
heaven and earth. The dawn is also a maiden, Eos: she drives
a rose-coloured chariot drawn by white horses. She sets out
before the sun, he following after: night and sleep fly before
her and the stars disappear.

The great sea has its greater spirit, the god Poseidon, 'the
mighty shaker of the shores'—'the azure-haired', so called
because the blue waves leap about his head as he rises from the
sea. In his hand he bears his trident, or three-pronged fork,
with which he rules the waves.

The greater gods live upon Mount Olympus. Those who
have climbed this tall mountain say that the snow lies unmelted
on its top even in the heats of July: but the old Greeks said
than an eternal spring reigned there, and there dwelt a marvel-
lous company of gods and goddesses who ruled the fates of men.
Father of them all was Zeus, the Roman Jupiter, whose voice
was the thunder and whose weapon was the lightning. He was
supposed to sit on an ivory throne with an eagle at his feet.
The queen of heaven was called Hera. She was a beautiful and
often an angry queen. When she wished to punish or to help
one of her favourites among men she would rush down from
the heavens like a falling star. The beautiful Phoebus Apollo
was the god of music and poetry and all the arts that go to make

life beautiful. He was much loved of the Greeks. Then there was the goddess of love and the noble goddess of wisdom, the god of wine and merriment and many more. Indeed it might be said that for every strong feeling of the heart and mind the Greeks imagined a radiant living spirit from whom it proceeded. The spirits of awe, love, anger, beauty, wisdom, and many more, were given a human form and fairy powers. Gods and goddesses these wonderful creatures were called, and on Mount Olympus was their home, whence they ruled the affairs of men. There they sat in their eternal spring, never growing older, feasting on nectar and ambrosia, the sweetest of food and drink—often laughing, often angry and quarrelsome, and often behaving in a very queer way indeed.

These were the beliefs of the very first of all the heroes, the mighty Heracles (or Hercules, as it is spelt in the Latin) about whom I am going to tell you, and whose story is one of the most wonderful in the world.

Try now to imagine a Grecian hall, the hall of a chieftain in the dusk of a winter evening. The hall is built with a foundation of stone, in which are grooved sockets holding the smooth round trunks of pine trees that stand like pillars down the centre of the hall, and at the sides lean towards the centre beam. In the middle of the hall is the open hearth, on which a fire of logs is kindled, smelling sweet and burning bright. How much the Greeks loved the hearth and the hearth fire it is hard for us now to tell. They reverenced the spirit of the hearth, and the hours passed around it were the sweetest in their lives. Picture them now seated about it: the children have had their supper of cakes and goats' milk and honey, for then as now the bees of Greece were busy, and there was plenty of honey to be had.

The children have bright, eager faces; they are hardy and strong, trained to bear pain bravely, tanned from the open air, boys and girls alike used to running and racing; and the boys, besides, are trained to use the bow and dart the spear, trained to ride and to speak and sing. Round about the fire sit the elders, grown men and women, and youths and maidens; and the boys and girls sit or lie at their parents' feet. They are brightly clad in robes and tunics, home-woven and home-dyed in good bright colours. The servants are there too, listening as well as the rest, and all the women have the distaff in their hand and spin as they listen.

The children's eyes are fixed on the bard or minstrel, whose head is a storehouse of wonderful tales. He wears a beard, and perhaps he is blind, as was old Homer, the greatest minstrel of them all. With him is his companion, a youth who holds in his hand a small harp and whose fingers are already playing skilfully among the strings.

'Tell us the story of Heracles,' cry the children, and the blind minstrel rises and lifts his hand; the harper sounds his strings, and in a sweet, sonorous voice the minstrel begins to chant.

HERACLES, son of Alcmena and of the mighty Zeus himself, was born to a noble house of Thebes. Such a babe for strength and beauty had never before been seen: the goddess Hera was jealous of him, and in anger she sent two snakes to devour him. Heracles and his brother Iphicles lay in the cradle in the hall, when silently the two bright, scaly snakes came gliding towards them, their heads lifted up, their forked tongues darting from their open mouths.

The children started at the sight, and Iphicles filled the hall with his shrieks; but the babe Heracles felt no fear, nor was fear ever destined to meet him in the way. In his two fists he seized the necks of the two snakes and strangled them, while they wreathed themselves about him. From all sides of the house the attendants came running, alarmed by the shrieks of Iphicles, and before their eyes was the awful sight—the child in his triumph.

After this act it was the belief of all that a great destiny lay before the boy. No one that saw his size and strength and beauty but was amazed; and for wit and daring there was none that came near him. Knowing then his greatness, in nothing did his mother spare to prepare him for the hero's life. Castor taught him how to fight, Eurytus how to shoot with a bow and arrows, Autolycus to drive a chariot, Linus to play on the lyre and Eumolpus to sing. As soon as he was a youth grown he became the pupil of the Centaur Cheiron; his companions were the sons of princes, the greatest in the land, but he outstripped them all.

Hardly was he seventeen years of age when he came to his strength. Then he left Cheiron, his master, and became his own man. With his own hand he slew dangerous beasts, and helped the weak against the strong, so that everywhere his name was spoken of.

But a hard fate was now coming fast upon the hero. At the time of his birth, Zeus his father had promised the angry Hera that Heracles should be subject to the will of Eurystheus.

Eurystheus was Prince of Mycenae, a rich man, and jealous.

When he heard of the great deeds of the young Heracles he was half angry and half fearful, dreading his rising power. Therefore he sent a message to Heracles, bidding him to appear before him and perform the labours he had a right to command of him.

Heracles, when he received the message, was sorely taken aback. Proud of his strength, he returned word that he would not come at any man's bidding, neither would he perform the labours that were asked of him.

He thought himself safe: but the angry goddess Hera, who wished to see him humbled, heard his proud words. Quickly she darted from her home on Mount Olympus, and laying her hand upon him, smote him with madness. Then in his madness and strength he laid about him, dreaming all who came near were the friends and kinsmen of Eurystheus, and fearful were his deeds. Men, women and children fled before him and, wherever he came, that place was soon emptied of all save himself.

In time the madness passed away and Heracles came to himself. When men told him of the deeds that he had done, sorrow seized upon him. He went and hid himself from men and wandered in the desert: not yet could he bring himself to bend his proud spirit, to obey the will of the gods and serve Eurystheus.

One day while passing through a wild oak wood, he came upon a small temple sacred to Phoebus Apollo. Bowed down by the sufferings brought upon him by his rebellion, Heracles entered and prostrated himself. The priest who had charge of the temple was amazed to see so huge a figure of a man thus cast down before him. He drew near and spoke to him.

Now this priest was old and white-bearded and had great knowledge of the hearts of men. In two days' time, when Heracles departed from him, he was become another man. His many clustered locks were combed, his limbs bathed and refreshed. He wore a tunic of white linen, and upon his head was a crown of the leaves of the white poplar. At his shoulder was his bow and quiver of arrows and in his right hand he carried his knotted club. He had determined to obey the will of Zeus by submitting himself to Eurystheus.

THE NEMEAN LION

EURYSTHEUS, Prince of Mycenae, sat in his hall. The watcher at the city gates had brought him word that the greatest man that had ever been seen was upon the road and coming towards the city. He wore no mantle, said the watcher, and carried a knotted club in his hand. By the club Eurystheus knew the man. In haste he sat himself in his carved chair and called the stoutest men of his guard about him.

Albeit in his own hall and well defended, the heart of Eurystheus melted within him when he saw the huge shoulders and limbs of Heracles and marked the flashing of his eye and his stalking gait as he advanced.

Half in fear and half in hatred Eurystheus looked upon him, and Heracles, gazing upon the prince in his carved chair, liked not his countenance. Neither greeted the other in kindness, and without more ado Heracles spoke.

'Zeus is the master of all men,' said he, 'and I have found it ill to fight against him. Now I am come hither to perform any labour that may be laid upon me.'

'Cousin,' said Eurystheus, 'since the will of Zeus falls upon all alike, needs must that I lay some task upon you. And now I bethink me of a labour by which you may win great worship and renown. In the land of Argolis there is a wood in which hides a lion huge and fierce, a terror to the land. No shepherd is safe upon the hills, the flocks are destroyed, the very children are taken from their fathers' doors. Go then and destroy me this lion, and so fulfil the will of Zeus.'

Without a word Heracles turned from the presence of Eurystheus and stalked from the hall and out of the city gates. And Eurystheus laughed behind his hand as he went, for he knew that bow and arrow and spear were of no avail against the Nemean lion, so tough and mighty was his hide, so cunning was he in his ambushes.

Heracles travelled swiftly till he came within sight of the wood of Nemea; then, because the noonday sun was hot, he asked for shelter and a draught of milk in a peasant's hut and room to lay himself down to sleep.

'By Zeus,' said the peasant, staring, 'shelter you may have with a right good will, and a draught of milk I will not refuse you: nay, you shall have a pailful and welcome: but for room to lay yourself down, in good faith, you shall not have that, unless it will content you to lay your feet out of the door and your head out of the window.'

Heracles laughed a mighty laugh, and stooping his head low he entered the cool shelter. He drank the milk and ate some oaten cakes, and propping his back against the wall he stretched his legs along the floor and fell asleep. When he awoke the sun was low in the heavens and there was a small noise of talking within the hut. The peasant man was sitting by the crossed logs on the hearth; his elbows were on his knees, and his head on his hands, and he seemed to be weeping and complaining; and an old woman stood by his side that seemed to try to give him comfort. 'Nay, nay, be a man, son,' she said. 'Never take on so for a maiden. There are others as fair as Callista.'

But the peasant man only groaned, but made no answer. Seeing him so heavy and sorrowful, Heracles raised himself up. 'What ails you, friend?' said he. The man only stared, but the old woman answered. 'My son has lost his bride, lord,' she said. 'It is now two moons since she went out to bring her two white heifers from the hill; but she has never come back.'

'She will never come again,' said the man, 'never. Her eyes were as bright as the morning, and she was but sixteen years old. My double curse on the beast that took her life.'

'What beast?' said Heracles. 'The lion, lord,' answered the woman. 'Up yonder in the wood of Nemea is his den. Every evening he is hunting, and every night not one but many fall his prey. Men, women and children—we do all quake for fear. The very sheep and bullocks will not fatten for the sound of his roars at evening.'

'I am come hither to destroy him,' said Heracles, rising up in his might. As they too rose up in amazement and stood staring upon him, evening came up and veiled the sky.

Heracles walked out of the hut, and the man and woman followed, crying upon him to let them serve and tend him and bathe his feet and bring him wine. But Heracles would not stay; no longer did he think of Eurystheus, nor of the burden that Zeus had laid upon him. The desire of a great deed was come upon him. To free the suffering people from this beast— this was work for a hero.

Above his head the stars were appearing in the purple sky. He went along paths that led through vineyards upward towards the wood of Nemea. Of a sudden he stood still. In his ear was a muttering like the distant sea on the stones of the shore: it was the far-away roaring of the lion. At the sound Heracles laughed, and standing still he took his bow from his shoulder, strung it, and tried the string, and fitted an arrow and slung his club from his neck by a loop. Then he went on and upward till he came to the borders of the wood. Then, coming to a standstill, he leaned his shoulders against an oak tree and stood still to listen, waiting for the moon to rise. For long he stood and heard no sound; then silently a shadow crossed the moonlight and before him Heracles saw the lion of Nemea, a monstrous beast, black and tawny, his nose snuffing in the air, his tail to the ground, his head turning this way and that. Heracles had fitted his heaviest arrow to his bow; quickly he drew it with his full strength, and the arrow sped towards the lion. It struck him full on the flank, but glided, shivering, off that tough and seasoned hide. The lion turned his head to look at his side and then smelt at the arrow. Heracles fitted another arrow that he called Swift Sailor to his bow, and sent that one humming upon the air towards the lion. As before, the arrow was broken and fell harmless to the ground. This time the lion uttered a roar that shook the air and bounded sideways, looking on his enemy. The joy of battle filled the heart of Heracles; with a shout he sprang from his hiding and ran towards the lion. For a moment the two enemies—the greatest of beasts and the greatest of men—glared upon each other; then the lion crouched for a spring. Quick as lightning Heracles hurled his knotted club, striking him upon the head;

but harder and more knotted was the skull of the lion within its vast shaggy mane of hair, and the club fell harmless to the ground. But for once such play was too rough for the beast; he rose up from his crouching and, tail to ground, he ran and escaped through the bushes. Heracles picked up his club and the broken arrows and hunted no more that night.

He found shelter for the asking at a peasant's hut, and dire were the tales he heard of the lion's nightly doings. But he bade the people who came round him in the early morning be of good cheer. He went out and bathed in a running stream and combed his long locks. When he had refreshed himself he bade one bring him a lyre, and with great beauty he played and sang, so that crowds came to hear and to rejoice in the hero. But some of the ruder men scoffed and said: 'Let him try his lyre on the hide of the Nemean lion.' 'Nay,' said an old woman, 'let him alone. The young man has skill; his strength will go the further.' Then Heracles exercised himself, and they watched him running and leaping and pitching the quoit; the young men and the maidens began to rouse themselves, and all fixed their hopes upon him.

An hour after noon Heracles went out to the hunt. That night the beast had killed on the side of a hill but a mile away, and feasted near a water-spring. The people led Heracles to the spot; then alone, he tracked the lion. Turning and winding through the mazes of the wood, it was late afternoon before he came upon his lair beneath an overhanging rock: deep woods were above and below. Many bones were strewed around the den of that bitter tyrant and the whole air was foul.

With a shout of joy Heracles bounded forward, casting his club; this time it smote the lion full on the brows as he raised himself on his forequarters. The blow notwithstanding, **like** lightning he crouched to spring; but even as he sprang Heracles steadied his limbs like two broad pillars, and opened his mighty arms. Like a thunderbolt the beast came upon him, but Heracles wreathed his fingers through the hair of his mane and caught him about the throat. Terrible was the deep breathing of the hero, the growling of the lion. Fearful was the struggle, but Heracles conquered; by main strength he squeezed the breath of life out of his enemy's throat, till it hung dead between his hands.

Throwing the mighty beast across his shoulders, Heracles made his way through the wood and down the hill.

With shouts the people began to run from all sides as they saw him descend the path through the vineyards. In crowds they ran about him, crying a thousand blessings upon him. They danced and shouted, and the women cried for joy.

'Heracles, stay with us, stay!' they cried. 'Rest yourself, hero! Let us bind up your wounds; here are wine and milk; lay down your burden that we may laugh at our old enemy dead.'

'Nay,' said Heracles, never stopping, 'the will of Zeus is laid upon me. I go to Mycenae.'

Towards evening the watcher upon the wall sent word to Eurystheus that a mighty crowd of people, dancing and running and playing upon flutes and wind instruments, was coming towards the gates, and in the middle of them was Heracles, bearing a lion upon his shoulders.

In haste Eurystheus summoned his guards to the hall and prepared himself to receive the hero. Through the open doors he came, a fearful figure; blood ran down from the wounds on his sides and shoulders where the lion had fixed his claws;

his face was flushed with heat and labour, and his eyes rolled in his head. Terrible and grim as was Heracles, more terrible and grim was the dead lion with his towering crest.

Eurystheus quaked for fear; he turned pale and shrank back among his guards.

Heracles marked him well, and a mighty contempt filled his heart.

He planted himself in the hall, and sent forth a shout of laughter. With his two hands he raised the lion, and with a mighty swing flung the carcass from him.

'Behold my labour accomplished!' he said. 'Now fear that, dead, which I feared not, living!'

With a crash the body of the huge beast fell upon the floor, and slid thundering along the well-smoothed oak beams. Eurystheus gave one glance and, turning his back, fled out of the hall.

THE LERNEAN HYDRA

A STRANGE thing now came to pass. It was Eurystheus that commanded and Heracles that obeyed. Yet Heracles through his courage became a free man and a hero, and Eurystheus became the slave of his fear.

He gave command that Heracles should never be allowed to pass the city gates; when he returned from his labours he was to be met outside the walls. Not content with this, he set about making for himself a hiding-place; he had a chamber dug underground, with a secret passage running between it and the hall. He caused his smiths to forge huge plates of brass and a brazen door and enormous nails, eighty-eight parts of copper to twelve of zinc. With these plates nailed to the walls he made himself a brazen chamber, that he might have a place of refuge wherein to hide from Heracles, should he chance to return victorious from his new labour. This time he thought he surely had him entrapped, for he sent him forth against the Lernean hydra.

The hydra was a hundred-headed snake, that lived in the marshes of Lerna. No one had as yet been able to destroy it, for as fast as one head was cut off, two new heads grew in its place.

Before he went Heracles thought long on this new task, and at last sent for his brother's son, a lad called Iolaus. Young as he was, this boy had a name for loyalty in friendship, and Heracles knew him to be staunch and fearless.

Together then they set out on the adventure. This time Heracles carried a long sword. When they reached the marshes they soon saw the tossing heads of the hydra. Every mouth was wide open and from every one came forth a poisoned breath.

From his bow Heracles sent forth a flight of arrows, each one following the other as swiftly as a string of wild swans across the sky. Each one flew to the mark and struck one of the hundred heads, but as each head dropped pierced by an arrow, two new ones grew in its place. Then Heracles rushed in with his club and laid about him with heavy blows, so swiftly dealt that Iolaus could see naught but a whirling circle above the dropping heads of the hydra. While Heracles fought this fierce battle, the angry Hera, fearful lest he should once more prevail, sent a huge crab against him that seized upon his heel.

Heracles drew back and destroyed this new enemy with a

blow of his club: whereupon Hera snatched up her favourite and placed him for a constellation in the sky.[1]

Finding the battle was in vain, Heracles gave over for the time and fell to thinking. Then he rose up and hewed down a willow tree, and bidding Iolaus cut it into logs and build up a monstrous fire, but not set it alight, he took his own way to a smith's. There he had fashioned for him two long iron rods with broad flattened tops.

Next morning early Iolaus lit the fire, and as soon as it was hot, Heracles thrust the broad ends of the iron rods into the flame. When they were heated red-hot, Heracles bade Iolaus take one and leave the other, and follow him to the combat.

With fearful fury Heracles fought the foul snake; and as each head was hewed off, Iolaus ran in and with his red-hot iron seared the root. All day the battle raged: Heracles and the young Iolaus were half blinded and half choked by the

[1] *Cancer*—the Crab.

poisonous breath of the dragon, but they still wrought on till evening. By sun-setting the last head fell; and the second labour was accomplished. A fearful sight were the marshes around. You would have said that a hundred men and a hundred dragons had been fighting there. Before they left the spot, Heracles unslung his quiver and dipped his arrows in the poison of the hydra. Then he and Iolaus found a pool of clear water and made haste to cleanse themselves; for indeed after their long toil they scarcely looked like men, and might not recognize each other. Then Heracles kissed the young Iolaus, and they lay down and slept.

In the morning came the people of Lerna who lived by the lake and the grove and on the banks of the two rivers between which lay the marshes, and great was the triumphing. The honour of the slaying was with Heracles, but Iolaus also won praise and renown. In after days a monument of stone was set up in his name, and all friends and lovers used there to speak their vows in remembrance of his fidelity.

Then, bearing the trophies of their victory, they took their way to the gates of Eurystheus. With him Heracles carried the poison of the hydra which, many years after and most strangely, was to prove fatal to himself.

The Stag of Aenoe

In Argolis there was a little village called Aenoe, which lay beneath a wooded hill. This place was famous because in the wood there haunted the most wonderful stag that had ever been seen. It was snow white; upon its head were branching horns of gold that shone in the sun, and its feet were of brass that made a ringing sound as they fled over rocks and upland paths more swiftly than the wind.

Now this stag was the beloved of Artemis, the hunting goddess. Eurystheus knew that this was so and that Artemis would be angry with any man who dared to chase her darling. Therefore he laid it upon Heracles that he should bring him the stag alive to the gates of Mycenae.

Now it chanced that Hephaistos, the Hammering God, had once given to Heracles a pair of brazen buskins, or high-thonged sandals. When Heracles heard of the brazen feet and amazing swiftness of the stag, he bound on his buskins of brass, and with his bow and quiver of fresh arrows, slight and without poison, he set forth for the wood of Aenoë.

It was not long before he put up the stag, for no covert could hide the brilliant creature, snow white and shining gold. For two days the stag ran and doubled through the woods and round the lake of its own place and home: then despairing of rest while this mighty hunter was behind, on the next day it sprang away and ran straight forward as swiftly as the wind toward the west.

And now it was brass buskin against brazen hoof. Their feet rang on the rocks and flew over mountain paths and fields. Both alike shod by the gods, they seemed never to tire. When night fell, each lay down in his place; when the morning dawned the stag looked for the hunter and the hunter looked for the stag. Then together they set off for the day's race.

In this manner they went on day after day till the days ran into weeks and the weeks into months. They came to the seas, and plunging in swam them together; right round the world they went and came again to Greece.

And now the stag went slow; he was wearied and his heart was sad; never now he knew could he escape this terrible hunter whose foot also was of brass. More and more slowly he went and great tears dropped from his eyes as the woods of Aenoë once more came in sight.

Heracles bounded forward, but even as he reached the side of the panting stag, a noise of hounds and a cry was heard within the wood. Out of the trees came the goddess Artemis herself, a half-moon bound upon her brows. She was running with her hounds, and behind her came flying her nymphs in a troop. When Heracles heard her cry and saw her running swiftly towards him with anger on her lips, he was seized with fear. He fell upon his knees, while the stag went and lay down at his mistress's feet.

'It is thou, then,' cried the goddess, 'that hast robbed me of my favourite! Had'st thou no fear?' She raised her bow with its arrow ready fitted and threatened: 'Knowest thou not that if I but touch this arrow's notch with intent to wound thee, thy life is spent?'

Heracles lifted his head and gazed at the pure and angry face of Artemis. 'Goddess,' he said, 'not of my own will, nor for my own pleasure, did I follow the stag. He is a right noble creature and hath run the world's round with me. Much joy I have had of him, as well as much labour, and not to save my right hand would I do him any hurt. Let me now, I pray you, obey the will of Eurystheus, whose commands are laid on me by Zeus himself. Let me take now the stag and show him to Eurystheus, and in all kindness bring him hither again.'

The goddess stooped and passed her hand over the noble neck of the creature that lay at her feet. She raised herself again and spoke with a calmer brow, looking kindly on the noble form of the hero as he knelt before her.

'Heracles,' she said, 'thou hast found favour with me. Thou hast a great spirit in a great body, and in the spirit is ever my delight. The will of Zeus must be obeyed, and for him that carries so dread a yoke upon his shoulders, the way must be made plain. Take now my deer and carry him to Eurystheus, but see thou bring him safely hither again.'

With a cry to her hounds, the goddess vanished and all her flying maidens. Willingly the stag went with Heracles to the gates of Mycenae. Eurystheus came outside the walls, and great was his wonder at the beauty of the stag, and very loth was he to let it go. But he needs must; and dangerous was the next labour he laid on Heracles, hoping greatly he might never see him again alive.

THE WILD BOAR OF ERYMANTHUS

IN a cavern at the foot of the cliff the wild boar of Erymanthus had his den. Out from the mouth of the den ran the boar's paths—some through the forests where he rooted for nuts and acorns, some to the water springs, and others, dangerous and steep, ran upwards to the mountains that towered above the cliff. To these mountain paths the boar betook himself when hotly pressed by hunters and their dogs.

This boar was of middle age, huge and dangerous, with immense tusks, one thrust of which had overthrown many a horseman, killing horse and man. Though so heavy, this boar could gallop faster than a horse: no man had as yet been able even to wound him, and because of him the forests and lands at the foot of the Erymanthean mountains were empty and uncultivated, for no man that cared for his life would venture therein.

This boar Eurystheus now commanded Heracles to bring him alive and unhurt: for he thought, the hero might slay him indeed, but no man, hero though he be, could take that beast unhurt and carry him so great a distance.

In good heart Heracles set out. Thrice he had conquered: not a soul that he met by the way but had heard of his deeds and blessed him as he went by. On his back were his arrows, in his hand was his club, and about his middle he had twisted cords for weaving into a net. Two tall, strong boarhounds followed him, well content to go out once more against their ancient enemy; indeed, on the day that Heracles came to Erymanthus, he might have had a hundred dogs for the asking, so eager were men to rid the country of its tyrant.

When the hounds struck the trail of the boar, they went first, and Heracles followed them. Like the wind they went, bounding so fast upon the trail that you might hardly mark them passing before they were gone. It was late autumn and the air was keen and sharp—good weather for the chase.

The boar was put up in a wood where he was seeking his midday meal. Good sport he made for the hounds and for Heracles, running all that day till evening. On the next day they hunted him again, following him hard and giving him no rest till they brought him to bay at the foot of his cliff. The steep bank was at his back, a brook ran down beside. Now the boar was very angry, and he was a fearful sight. With his forefeet he scraped up the earth; every now and then he turned and whetted his white tusks on the rock by his side.

The foam ran from his mouth; brave as they were, the hounds were afraid.

Heracles, shouting, cheered them on: they ran in obediently, but in a moment the boar had bitten the back of one across and ripped the other up, flinging him across the brook. Out from his hole he rushed and up a path leading between craggy rocks to the higher hills.

Now Heracles depended no more on hounds, but alone and on foot he followed the boar. Snow came down; sometimes the track was hidden, but he never stopped nor paused, and the heavy boar was wearied almost to death. Many a flight of arrows did Heracles draw upon him, but they slid off his sides. Many a time did the brazen club reach him, but his huge strength scarcely heeded the blows.

Though it was but late autumn among the oak woods at the foot of the mountains, above on the heights it was winter and the snow was deep. Sitting by the fire one night in a herdsman's hut, Heracles thought long and deeply. On rough ground the boar could beat him, galloping faster than he, and hurling himself through the under-bushes, while Heracles must stop to break a path. In his own den Heracles might not come near to him, so fierce were his rushes, so sharp his tusks.

On the other hand, the boar was short legged and heavier than Heracles. 'Therefore', thought the hero, 'my chance lies in the snow. The waddling boar may not come through what I can leap over. Tomorrow I will drive him up the mountains, and it will be a strange thing if I do not find a snow trap for him.' Heracles lay down and slept that night. In the morning early he took a pack of hounds and went after his stout enemy. With caution he hunted him, neither he nor his hounds coming near the boar, lest he should double back for the woods, but letting him run free and always heading him off till he took the upper paths. For five hours they ran till the dogs were tired, and Heracles gave them some rest. Above on the snowy slope the panting boar lay down to rest behind a rock. But soon Heracles had him up again, and fleetly running with his hounds to right and left, kept him still upward, and going for a steep mountain gorge, where Heracles knew the snow lay deep.

More and more slowly went the heavy boar, a moving black speck in the white snow. Many times he tried to break away for the lower paths, but Heracles and his dogs were ready for him, and the brazen club flew, turning him always upward till he entered the gorge and plunged into the deep snow.

Now Heracles laughed till the hills rang as he watched his enemy plunging and smothering. His net was ready; and when the boar's strength was spent he came near and wound it about him, marvelling as he did so at his huge size and his leathery hide and his bristles and his mighty tusks, and his little eyes in his hideous countenance. Because, for all that, he was an honest boar and had run well, kindly did Heracles address him while he bound him, struggling, in the net. Round them in a ring stood the hounds, yelling, and greatly longing to take vengeance on their now helpless enemy.

With might and main Heracles strove with the boar, and at length, using the whole of his terrible strength, he heaved the fearful monster on his back and, staggering as he went, took his way downward to the plains. He was followed by a shouting crowd till the night fell. In the early morning he came bearing his huge burden to the gates of Mycenae; now the watcher had left for a while his post on the walls, and Heracles stood within

the gates, and coming to the hall of Eurystheus, passed within
and stood and shouted.

From all sides ran the attendants and officers; then Heracles
could no longer forbear; he lowered the boar from his back and
slipped the net even as Eurystheus came into the hall. The
monster began to stir himself, and even as Eurystheus came
forward, he rolled upon his feet and stood snorting, ready to
rush. One look Eurystheus gave at his shining tusks, and then
turned and fled, leaving behind him the shout of Heracles'
great laughter. Eurystheus fled the faster, and coming to his
brazen chamber, ran within, shutting the mighty door with a
clang, and making it fast with bolts. Safe there, he thought
within how he would now humble Heracles. Hitherto he had
given him fair tasks by which he won worship and honour,
and the love and gratitude of the people: now he would find
for him a base task by which no honour could be got, but which
might for ever lower his pride. 'Let him laugh, then,' said
Eurystheus to himself, and as he spoke he smiled; in all the
polished walls of his brazen room the smile was repeated again.
But if Eurystheus had foreseen the future, he might have
paused. He was fast winning the undying hatred of those that
loved Heracles. One day the young Iolaus, faithful always in
his friendship, was to avenge the wrongs of Heracles by the
slaying of his oppressor.

THE AUGEAN STABLES

IN Elis there lived a prince called Augeas, who had many
thousands of oxen, sheep and goats. The stables in which all
these animals were housed had never been cleansed, and

because of this the name of Augeas was made a proverb throughout Greece.

The labours that Eurystheus had now devised for Heracles was that he should go to Elis and clean the stables of Augeas.

Heracles set forth once more: of no avail now were his arrows nor his brazen club, the weapons of a hero.

In two days' time he came to Elis, within sight of the valley where Augeas dwelt. Over the green meadows roamed thousands of oxen. Herds of goats were on the hillsides. Through the valley, like a silver thread, ran the River Peneus. The house of Augeas stood on higher ground, and below it, like a little town, were the long stables which sheltered his flocks.

Heracles laid down his club and sat himself on a rock, to consider. It was not the command of Eurystheus only that he must obey; it was the command of Zeus. After a while an idea came to him, and he rose up and descended into the valley, carefully considering the ground as he went.

By the time he reached the dwelling of Augeas, the cloud had gone from his face. Augeas was a long-bearded man, hoary and grey. He sat in his chair and looked over the valley, and two noble sons stood by him.

'By the command of Zeus, I am come hither to clean your stables, Augeas,' said Heracles. 'This is indeed pleasant news for my ears, hero,' replied Augeas. 'But I fear me it is beyond the power of man. Five score men have laboured for many moons, but the stables are worse than before.'

'Nevertheless', said Heracles, 'I have a mind to clean them. And if I do so, what reward may I ask of you, Augeas?' 'The tenth part of the flocks and herds will I gladly give,' said Augeas.

'Agreed,' said the hero. 'And now let your herdsmen drive out every bull and goat from the stables and out of the valley, and up to the higher pastures, for when Heracles goes a-cleaning, the very earth will shake!' and he shouted with laughter. Then Phyleus, son of Augeas, ran to the side of Heracles, and took his hand, and prayed him for his friendship; and Heracles gave it him straightway.

Heracles asked for an axe and a spade, and they were brought; and all stood to see him go down to the stables, and great was the merriment. But Heracles stalked away through the valley with never so much as a glance at the stables. Away up to the foot of the hills he went, following the banks of the little River Peneus.

Coming to a spot which he had marked, where the river ran through a grove, he threw off the lion skin from his shoulders, and fell to work. First he cut down a tree and hewed it into logs; then with his spade he dug a channel, and led it into an old watercourse that he had spied. He worked so fast that the clods flew and the rocks rolled, and soon all was ready, and a new bed laid for the river. Then with his main strength he heaved his logs across the river and piled great stones and earth above them, and on the top of the dam he himself leaped to hold all steady against the flood.

The river came down fast and rose angrily against its barriers. Heracles looked upwards and saw where it came springing down from the hills like a chain of flying nymphs with silver hair. He raised his hand and cried:

'Forgive, oh fair Peneus, that I have laid the cruel task upon thee which was commanded of me by the will of Zeus. Dire necessity compels us both. Flow but this one day in a new channel, cleanse me thine own valley, and at evening thou shalt return to thy well-loved couch. Moreover, a golden obolus and a polished cup of olive wood I will lay therein as recompense.'

When the angry river heard these words it rose no more upon the dam, but turned and flowed obedient in the new channel, carrying down earth and stones and gravel, boiling and fretting as it ran. What a shouting and a running to and fro and a driving off of cattle there was in the valley as the river came raging down! Afar off Heracles stood and watched laughing, the lion skin upon his shoulder, his club in his right hand.

Toward evening, with grateful thanks and duly paid offering, he turned back the river into its own bed where once more it flowed rejoicing. Then he took his way back to the dwelling of Augeas.

In the fresh-cleansed stables Heracles found him standing on the wholesome floor of earth and gravel which Peneus had left behind him.

'Your stables are cleansed, Augeas,' said Heracles. 'Where is now my reward?'

'Go ask the river, Heracles,' said Augeas. 'It is to the water I must pay a tenth part of my flocks. It is Peneus that has done the work, not thou, and not a goat nor an obolus shalt thou have.'

When Heracles heard these words, the veins of his forehead rose and swelled with the anger that he felt. But Phyleus stood out and said: 'This is an unjust decision, oh my father. The stables are cleansed, and it is Heracles that has cleansed them. Give him now his reward.'

But Augeas would not listen: his pride and delight lay in

the huge number of his flocks; cleanliness and honour were of small account to him. He muttered in his beard, and turned his back on the hero.

Then Heracles cried aloud and said : 'Beware of me from this day, Augeas. You have saved the tenth part of your herds, but look that this deed does not cost you your high seat in your own hall.'

And so in after years it befell, for Heracles went to war with Augeas and slew him, and placed Phyleus his son in his seat. But some say that Phyleus would not sit in his father's chair, but went away and founded a city by himself.

THE STYMPHALIAN BIRDS

HERACLES had now proved himself wise as well as strong and fearless. He was the first hero of his time, and both gods and men were with him, as he was soon to prove.

The next task that was laid upon him by Eurystheus was that he should destroy the fearful birds that infested a valley hard by the lake of Stymphalus.

With a light heart Heracles now set forth, thinking it a small matter to shoot down a flight of birds. He took in his hand his well-tried bow and a quiver of poisoned arrows, and merry was the way to him.

Even when he came nigh the place and saw the narrow, stony valley and the dark rocks, and the huge birds perched like sentinels, with round, golden eyes and hooked bills, he was in no wise daunted. He fitted an arrow to his bow and walked carefully forward to make sure what kind of task was this he had to do.

The narrow valley was foul with bones and full of a most evil odour. There were the bones of men and women and children, as well as of sheep and goats, and Heracles had need to pick his steps if he would not tread on them. In the rocks above were the nests with the downy headed young looking out from them. Many large birds were on the wing flying to and fro, all now staring at the man who had invaded their safe kingdom.

Heracles had not thought there were so many: he retreated backward to the mouth of the valley, looked well to his quiver of arrows and made ready his bow. Then with wonderful swiftness he began to slay: arrow flew after arrow, and for every poisoned arrow a bird fell. Those that were still unhurt rose with loud screamings and with clapping wings into the air. Like a black cloud they descended at once and all together, and fearful was their onset.

To Heracles it seemed as though the sky were grown suddenly black. With harsh screams the birds attacked him; they beat upon him with their wings; they tore him with their talons; they wounded him with their powerful beaks, that aimed always at his eyes. In spite of the hard strokes of his whirling club, the birds were so many that he was harder pushed than ever before. As the wounded ones drew off, those that were wheeling overhead fell upon him till he was choked, stifled and wounded, and in danger of his life.

Then a strange thing happened; in the midst of the furious battle a sudden peace fell upon him. Wounded and panting he looked upward, and over him spread a golden shield. Beside him stood the noble form of Pallas Athené, with helmeted head and firm, resplendent countenance. Awe filled the hero's

heart as he gazed. 'Shoot, Heracles,' said the goddess. 'Perform thy task. My shield keeps thee. Thy valour has deserved my protection.'

Thus was the battle decided. Protected by the goddess, the twanging bow and poisoned arrows of Heracles left not a bird alive in all the Stymphalian valley.

THE WILD BULL OF CRETE

AT this time King Minos reigned in Crete, a fair and rich island round which flowed the waves of the sea. Minos loved the sea, and honoured Poseidon, the sea god; so he prayed of him to send some fair beast that he might sacrifice upon his altars. At the prayer of Minos the blue waves opened, and there came up out of the sea a milk-white bull. He was the greatest and most splendid bull that had ever been seen. On his forehead were a hundred short and snowy curls, his horns were short and polished, his head was broad, and his snow-white hair lay in curls upon his flanks. Such a bull King Minos had never seen: it was too much; he could not sacrifice such a creature. Secretly he kept him, and sacrificed another in his place.

But it is impossible to deceive the gods. Poseidon knew all and was angry. In revenge he struck the bull with madness, and in place of being a treasure to his possessor, he became a curse. No walls could hold him, no fences or bars; his bellow was heard through the island; he seemed to be filled with a rage for destruction. With his broad forehead he pushed down, and with his horns he tossed and tore all that came in his way, and not a man, woman or child in all the island of Crete but lived in fear.

This bull Eurystheus now commanded Heracles to bring back alive to Greece.

Heracles took boat and crossed the sea, and much he rejoiced when he saw his new enemy.

'Ha ha!' he said and laughed. 'We shall have many a noble game, thou and I. Tame as a dog thou shalt return with me to Greece.'

Thereafter the white bull did no more damage in the island of Crete, for from sunrise to sunset he hunted Heracles and was hunted by him. Merry were the wrestlings they had together and the trials of strength and speed. But always Heracles was victor; and when at length he made ready to sail back to Greece, tame as a lamb the great bull followed him on board.

The Mares of Diomede

In Thrace at this time there ruled a tyrant called Diomede, so cruel and so barbarous that he kept a herd of mares which he fed on human flesh.

These mares Eurystheus commanded Heracles to bring captive to the walls of Mycenae.

As Heracles journeyed thither his rage and indignation rose against so horrible a tyrant, and he determined to destroy him. Making a halt therefore, he sent to summon the bravest and trustiest of his friends, and first of all he sent to the noble Iolaus. At once and from all quarters the young men came flocking, all of them armed, all eager to attend upon Heracles, who was by so much the greatest of them all.

Like a small army they marched together upon Thrace. Speaking peace everywhere to the people, they went up only against Diomede himself; and almost without a blow they took him, and alive.

Diomede was a young man, strong and cruel. He was brought, bound, before Heracles, who, before punishing him, cried out in a loud voice, and asked if there were any there that desired that mercy should be shown to the tyrant. But no one answered and begged for his life.

Then Heracles said: 'It is fitting that the same mercy should be shown to Diomede that he has shown to others. Let us know if the tale that is told of him be indeed a true one. Let him be thrown to his mares, and see will they spare him. They, not we, will condemn and punish him, if the truth has been told. We desire only that justice shall be done.'

In a bare desert field, high-walled, the mares were kept.

Diomede, who now in his turn was struck with mortal fear, was thrust within. The herd of mares came down upon him; they opened in a circle, as though preparing for some strange dance; they backed down upon him, and screaming, struck him with their hoofs; then turning, ran in upon him with bared teeth and ears laid back—and there was an end of the tyrant.

Now the task laid upon Heracles and his friends was to take the mares alive; therefore they entered the field, each one armed with a club and a running noose. As they neared the herd, they saw that the mares were skeleton thin; their bones showed through their raw and ragged hide, their eyes rolled red and their great teeth shone from beneath the back-drawn lips. But without fear or hesitation Heracles and his friends awaited their rush and, with a blow of the club and a throw of the tight-strangling noose, each one led a mare captive behind him.

When they arrived before the gates of Mycenae, Eurystheus came forth strongly guarded to see the mares and listen to the tale of Diomede. 'And it is not possible, Eurystheus,' said Heracles, 'that such beasts should remain alive, a horror in the eyes of men. Let them be sent to the slopes of Mount Olympus, where man's foot never treads, and there let the wild beasts or the lightning of the gods destroy them.' And so it was done.

The Girdle of Hippolyte

Eurystheus was now more than ever full of fear. 'What!' said he to himself. 'He begins to lead an army. This time his task shall take him so far that he shall never come back, else I shall be asked to behold the whole land of the Hellenes rising at his back.' The labour that he now laid upon Heracles was that he should travel eastward till he found the land of the Amazons, and then that he should take from the queen her girdle and bring it to the gates of Mycenae.

Now the Amazons were a nation of women who lived across the sea, far away toward the rising sun. They were fierce and warlike and great haters of men. They were most skilful archers, and so cunning in their fashioning of bows that no one could shoot against them, and if any man of the Greeks had a powerful far-carrying bow, he called it Amazonian.

But Eurystheus made a great mistake when he sent Heracles against Hippolyte as an enemy. For Heracles was not only brave and strong and a great fighter, but he had a wise head; he was prudent, courteous, a lover of justice and of a noble mind. Also he was fair to look upon and could make the evening hours pass cheerily by with tales and songs and the music of his lyre. Also the renown of his valiant deeds travelled on before him so that he found friends awaiting him, so much do men and women honour a hero.

Many wonders did Heracles see—the army of women, clad in white tunics, strong, bold and tall, carrying each one of them a great bow and a quiver of arrows. He saw their second army of trained horsewomen, armed with spear and shield. He visited their city, Themyscyra, and saw their strange customs and heard their laws.

At last Hippolyte the queen sent for him and straightway gave him her friendship. On three sides of her palace hall stood her armed guards, young women chosen for their stature and strength. She herself was tall and splendidly dressed in a robe of golden tissue. Her long hair flowed on her shoulders, bound with a jewelled band. Her bearing and her manner were haughty, but made sweet to Heracles by a smile of welcome.

'Hail, hero,' she said. 'Long and wonderful have been the tales that have been told to me of thy most fearful labours. No shoulders less than thine could have borne so heavy a yoke. Now to the tale of thy deeds thou canst add thou hast conquered Hippolyte. Take now from the hand of friendship what neither force nor craft could ever have won. Of my own will I give thee the girdle of Hippolyte.'

So speaking, the noble queen loosed from her waist her girdle of gold, broad and deep and set with shining gems of every colour. Heracles knelt upon one knee and took it straight from her hand, honouring her that gave it.

In truth it was a bitter moment to him when, at the end of his journeyings, he must needs surrender this priceless gift to Eurystheus.

Geryon the Monster

Great was the joy of Eurystheus over the golden girdle, but bitter was his anger at the easy victory of Heracles.

'I will send him out against one who has no love for the lyre and is scarce likely to be conquered by his handsome face,' said he, and commanded Heracles to take ship and sail to Gades, there to destroy the monster Geryon and bring back his flocks.

Now Geryon had three heads and three bodies, but stood upon two legs. When Heracles landed upon the sea beach, and saw this monster come walking over the hill, with his three mouths bellowing and his six arms whirling, while his two-headed dog ran doubly howling on before, he was seized with so huge a laughter that he stood helpless upon the shore. This had nearly been his destruction and an end of him, for the six hands of Geryon plucked six huge stones and hurled them down upon the hero, who ran backward into the waves to escape them. Then swiftly Heracles strung his bow and sent three poisoned arrows on their way, one for each of the bodies of Geryon, so that the monster was fain to lie down and die. After that Heracles slew his two-headed dog and his hideous herdsman and drove away all his herds.

The Golden Apples of the Hesperides

HERACLES had now proved himself invincible, untiring, the most dreaded of heroes; and Eurystheus resolved to send him to the very ends of the earth to be rid of him. He desired him to bring back to Greece the golden apples of the Hesperides which grew in the garden beyond the oceans which Perseus had visited. This garden was full of fruits of the most delicious kind, and was guarded by dragon Ladon who never slept, night or day.

The tree on which grew the apples was tended by three splendid nymphs clad in rose and gold blue, the colours of dawn, and called the Hesperides. Heracles, not knowing where to find the gardens, journeyed and wandered far, till one day, walking by a river bank in the land of Italy, he spied the river nymphs at play and begged them to tell him the way.

'That we cannot tell you,' cried they. 'You must go and seek old Nereus, who sits by the shore of the Aegean Sea. You will know him by his long beard and his azure hair. His fifty daughters dance around him and sing in choruses together,

Evagora, Evarne, Glauconome . . .' But though sweet were the river nymphs' voices, Heracles could not wait while they sang the fifty names of the Nereides.

In a grotto by the sea he found old Nereus, and the cunning old god did not wish to answer, so he changed his shape and became a black lobster that sat and blinked on the sand. But Heracles seized him and made as though he would dash him upon a rock, and in a moment old Nereus became a huge dun bull fearful to behold. Heracles made one stride and got him by the horns, and so powerful was the hero's grip that Nereus took his own shape again and freely answered him.

Heracles followed all his counsels, and at last came to the huge mountain in Africa, on the top of which Atlas knelt, supporting all the heavens upon his shoulders.

Heracles climbed the mountain and begged of Atlas to tell him the way to the garden. 'Nay, brother,' said Atlas, 'I will rather fetch the apples for thee myself. Kneel down by me that I may shift the heavens on to thy back; thou art strong enough.' Heracles kneeled down and Atlas shifted his load and went merrily away to find the Hesperides. Soon he came back again with three golden apples.

'To Eurystheus of Mycenae these golden apples must be given, sayest thou?' he said. 'I will myself take them to him. So many years have I held up the heavens on my back, I am grown weary of the work. Thou, Heracles, art young and strong, and may well perform this task in my place.'

Heracles considered within himself. The work was odious to him; he was wellnigh crushed with the weight of the heavens, but he spoke cheerfully.

'Willingly, brother. But the heavens are a heavy burden to

carry and in truth they gall my back, which is not used to the work. Relieve me but for a moment while I make a pad for my shoulders on which the heavens may rest.'

Atlas knelt down and took the world on his back once more. Heracles picked up the apples and fled away, never looking behind him till he came to Greece, and surrendered the apples to Eurystheus at the gates of Mycenae.

The Dog Cerberus

Eurystheus sat in his brazen room, considering. Only one more labour remained for Heracles to do, and then he would be a free man. One last chance was left to Eurystheus of getting rid of his enemy, who seemed but to grow the stronger for his trials. There was one place only from which no human soul— hero or king—ever came back; that was the underworld, where the spirits of the dead lived and wandered in an eternal twilight. Therefore to Hades, the underworld, Heracles should go and bring to earth Cerberus, the dog that guarded those fearful regions.

Without fear or hesitation Heracles set out on his fearful journey. Among the mountains of Arcadia a cold and poison- ous spring issues from the earth, flows as a river for a little space and then plunges downward into depths below that are unknown and feared of mortals. So bitter is this river, called Styx, that it consumes iron and breaks any vessel that is cast into it. Into these waters Heracles plunged, and following them downward soon arrived at the Stygian Lake. By its dark shores in the twilight waited Charon, the ancient boatman who ferried the souls of the dead across to Hades. He was a strong old man with a hideous countenance, and a long white beard. His garment was ragged and dirty and his forehead covered with wrinkles. He looked on Heracles with his piercing eyes. 'Thou art living,' said he. 'Get thee from here. My boat is for the dead.'

'Nay,' said Heracles, 'thou must ferry me across. By the will of Zeus I go to bring Cerberus up to the light of day, even to the gates of Mycenae.'

'Where is thy golden bough?' asked Charon. 'Without it thou canst not pass, but must wander by these shores a hundred years.'

'No golden bough have I brought,' said Heracles, 'but yet this lake of Styx will I pass.' And so saying he leaped into the boat, and the terrified old man gave way and ferried him over, grumbling to himself: 'Pluto will have me in prison for this; no mortal must cross without the golden bough.'

At the gates of Hell waited the three-headed Cerberus with awful jaws. But Heracles was no dead fluttering shade; and before this most terrible of mortals Cerberus drew backwards till he came to Pluto's hall, where he lay down at Pluto's feet. Now Pluto was King of Hades. He sat high on a throne of sulphur, and four rivers ran from beneath his feet. He was a hard-hearted and inexorable god, of a grim and dismal countenance. Beside him sat Persephone, his earth-born wife, fair and sad and pale, always longing for the flowery valleys of earth and the light of the sun and the sound of the laughter of the living.

'Hail, Pluto,' said Heracles, addressing the grim god. 'I am commanded by Eurystheus to bring up Cerberus from this underworld and into the eye of day.'

'Thou art Heracles,' said Pluto, 'but thou shouldest be called madman too, to make such a request. Who then would guard the gates of my kingdom?'

'Pluto, thou hast many servants to do thy work. But as for me, I am alone to do the work which Zeus has laid upon me. Eleven labours have I performed; I have been to the ends of the earth, and felt the weight of the heavens on my back, and now this last labour will I perform, if I have to pull down the walls of Hades and perish myself in the undertaking.'

'Take Cerberus, if thou canst,' said Pluto, 'but thou must bring him hither again.'

Then Heracles seized the monster and dragged him up from Hades all the way. So fearful did he look beneath the eye of the sun that Eurystheus gladly sent him from his sight. Heracles, therefore, led him downward again, and pleased was the willing monster to behold the fearful gates, the thousand thousand gliding shadows of the dead, and the dim uncertain light of his own land.

Then Heracles returned to earth. The air and the sunlight seemed sweeter to him than ever before, for now after long labour he was free, and every task had been accomplished. He had subdued himself to follow the will of Zeus, and found it led him to honour. His feet were firmly set now on the hero's path; the grateful thanks and praises of the Hellenes were loud in his ears. Many and many an adventure of joy was before him. Freed from the yoke of Eurystheus he stood up the greatest man in Greece. In the distant years, death, which comes to all, indeed awaited him; but after death there awaited him the immortality of Mount Olympus, the companionship of the gods and an unforgotten name.

Such were the tales that the Greek children of long ago listened to by the hearth fire. For one tale that you may read in the book of 'Heroes' there were many a hundred told in those faraway days. Old Homer tells a thousand in his *Iliad,* and a thousand more in his *Odyssey.*[1] Turn to any page of Homer and the names of heroes shine from it like stars in the sky. In those pages you read how dear was valour to the heart of the Greeks. With loving pleasure Homer writes of his great men. He tells you of the heroes rising from sleep. Agamemnon, the leader of the Greeks, lies sleeping in his tent and dreams a strange dream:

> Starting he woke, and seeming still to hear
> The warning voice divine, with hasty leap
> Sprang from his bed and sat. His fleecy vest
> New-woven, elegant, he first put on,
> And his broad mantle—braced his sandals, next,
> To his unsullied feet, and slung his sword,
> With silver studs adorned.

Homer writes the Tale of Hector, 'valiant Hector, huge',

> bearing in his gripe
> Eleven cubits' length of massy spear,
> The burnish'd head bound fast with circling gold.

He sings of

> Terrific Ajax, bulwark of the Greeks,
> Smiling ferocious, with impatient haste
> Striding, and brandishing his massy spear.

He sings of Achilles with his golden locks and stormy spirit, which yet he has the strength to govern as Pallas Athené commands him, saying:

> Who hears the gods, the gods hear also him.

[1] You may find these tales retold by Andrew Lang in *The Adventures of Odysseus.*

He sings of Odysseus, the wise and cunning of wit, and of his endless wanderings by sea and land and his adventures with enchantresses and monsters. Perhaps the best of all the Greek tales is the story of Odysseus and the Cyclops, a vast one-eyed monster, who feeds on human flesh. Driven by contrary winds, Odysseus and his companions land on the rocky coast of Sicily below Mount Etna, where they fall into the hands of the Cyclops, and are pent in his cavern.

This is how Odysseus himself tells a part of the story:

> Soon as we came into this craggy place,
> Kindling a fire, he cast on the broad hearth
> The knotty limbs of an enormous oak,
> Three wagon-loads at least, and then he strewed
> Upon the ground, beside the red fire-light,
> His couch of pine leaves; and he milked the cows,
> And pouring forth the white milk, filled a bowl
> Three cubits wide and four in depth, and bound it
> With ivy wreaths; then placed upon the fire
> A brazen pot to boil, and made red hot
> The points of spits. And when this hideous cook
> Had made all ready, he seized two of us
> And killed them in a kind of measured manner;
> For he flung one against the brazen rivets
> Of the huge cauldron, and seized the other
> Firm by the ankle, and knocked out his brains
> Upon the sharp edge of the craggy stone,
> And put him down to roast. The other's limbs
> He chopped into the cauldron to be boiled.
> And I, with the tears raining from my eyes,
> Stood near the Cyclops, ministering to him;
> The rest, in the recesses of the cave,
> Clung to the rocks like bats, bloodless with fear.

How Odysseus, with the rest of his companions, revenges himself on the Cyclops, and how he escapes from the terrible cavern, you must read for yourselves in Homer's story.

When you are older, you will discover other heroes in Greek history: heroes in patriotism, heroes in art and in poetry, heroes in thought, as well as makers of lovely forms, from whom the world is still learning. Then you will at last rightly understand how great is our debt to the valiant race of the heroes of old Greece.